THE SOUL'S
QUEST FOR
GOD

Also in the R. C. Sproul Library

The Hunger for Significance

The King without a Shadow

The Glory of Christ

THE SOUL'S QUEST FOR
GOD

SATISFYING *the* HUNGER *for*
SPIRITUAL COMMUNION *with* GOD

R.C.
SPROUL

PUBLISHING
P.O. BOX 817 • PHILLIPSBURG • NEW JERSEY 08865-0817

Unless otherwise indicated, all Scripture quotations are from the King James Version.

Printed in the United States of America

Library of Congress Cataloging-in-Publication Data

Sproul, R. C. (Robert Charles), 1939–
    The soul's quest for God : satisfying the hunger for spiritual communion / R. C. Sproul.
        p. cm. — (R. C. Sproul library)
    Originally published: Wheaton, IL : Tyndale House, c1992.
    Includes bibliographical references and index.
    ISBN 0-87552-706-X
    1. God—Worship and love. 2. Desire for God. I. Title.

BV4817S64 2003
248.2—dc21

2003046289

For Aurelius, Thomas,
Martin, Jean, and Jonathan
—who understand the soul's quest.

CONTENTS

PREFACE

Something is missing. It is missing from the life of the church. It is absent from the normal Christian life. What is missing is a depth of spiritual communion with God. Worship is unsatisfying to multitudes, and the Christian life is often marked more by a sense of the absence of God than a vital sense of his presence.

There is a spot deep within our souls that is hungry and not being fed. There is a place in our hearts that is thirsty, and no one gives us to drink. There is a naked corner of our spirits that no one offers to clothe.

Yet it is the work of Jesus to feed the hungry, give drink to the thirsty, and cover the naked. He does not fail in these endeavors. He is as able to provide physical and spiritual food for us as he was for the five thousand. He is as able to give us living water as he was for the woman of Sychar. He is as able to clothe us as he was the demoniac of the Gadarenes. Jesus has not changed. Nor has he moved and failed to supply a forwarding address. We are the ones who have moved. We neglect him and his Word and wonder why we are hungry, thirsty, and naked.

Christ has promised that all who seek him will surely find him. But we must seek him.

This book is about a quest. It is about the most important quest of our lives. It is the soul's quest for God. The quest is for the wellspring of life, for the taste of the sweetness of honey in our mouths, and for the divine light that alone can illumine our darkest chambers.

We will examine the biblical pattern for spiritual growth with assistance from some of the spiritual giants of church history. We will look at biblical models of spiritual maturity and consider the mysterious character of the human soul itself. We will seek to discover something about the nature of the soul, its value, and most important, how it is nurtured. We will consider barriers to the soul's quest, particularly those that stand between us and assurance of salvation.

Finally, we will consider the ultimate destination

of the soul, the prize that awaits those who earnestly seek after God, namely the beatific vision, the blessed vision of God himself.

Special thanks are in order for Wendell Hawley, who suggested this work, and for Maureen Buchman and Donna Mack, who helped in the preparation of the manuscript. Thanks also to my friends at Heathrow, who protected my privacy while I labored.

1

RESTLESS HEARTS

O Lord, Thou hast created us for Thyself
and our hearts are restless until they find
their rest in Thee.[1]

*T*HESE IMMORTAL LINES FROM THE
pen of Aurelius Augustine capture the deepest sentiments of every Christian. In his autobio-
graphical classic, *The Confessions*, Saint Augustine
traced his own personal spiritual pilgrimage. Augustine revealed in prose what John Bunyan depicted in
allegory—the progress of the soul as it moves toward spiritual rest in Christ.

Christianity engages the mind. Its revelation is
designed by God for cognitive understanding. It
calls believers to a new kind of living with its radically transcendent view of life and the world. Yet
beyond all of this the Christian faith is an *affaire de
coeur*, an "affair of the heart."

Another work I published[2] stresses a strange paradox of Christianity: At one and the same time the
Christian faith bears a primacy of the intellect and a

primacy of the heart. To say that there are two primacies at the same time jars the brain and alerts the thinker to the presence of a bald contradiction. Two primacies? How can anything have a double primacy? Does not the word *primacy* connote something that is alone and singularly primary?

Indeed it does. At first glance this appears to be a contradiction, but it is really a paradox. A paradox differs from a contradiction at precisely this point: Upon closer examination the paradox yields a resolution. No such resolution can ever be found for a bona fide contradiction.

If we were to say that Christianity has two primacies at the very same time *and* in the very same relationship, we would indeed be wandering from the path of cogency and sobriety. There would be a contradiction.

However, when we say that Christianity has a primacy of the mind and of the heart we are saying that the twin primacies coexist at the same *time*, but not in the same *relationship*.

On the one hand, Christianity has a primacy of the mind with respect to order or sequence. Nothing can be in the heart that is not first in the mind. Our hearts cannot be inflamed about something we know not of. Unless we know God deeply, we cannot love him deeply. A faint understanding of God is enough to begin the heart to stir. Emotions may be kindled by the slightest acquaintance with the majesty of Christ. But for that spark to rise into a consuming and lasting fire, our knowledge of him must increase.

To know him is to love him. Therefore, deepening knowledge must precede deepening affection. The mind comes first; it is primary for our faith.

On the other hand, there is a primacy of the heart. This primacy is not one of order or sequence, but one of *importance*. Many have accumulated a storehouse of theological knowledge, yet their hearts remain sterile and cold. History is replete with evidence of scholars who distinguished themselves with erudition used in the cause of unbelief. A creed cannot save anyone. It is with the heart that we believe unto salvation. A necessary element of saving faith is affection for Christ. A lot of knowledge with no love is worthless. A little knowledge coupled with great affection is far preferable.

God is most pleased when we pursue *both* primacies. The pursuit of the knowledge of God is insufficient. It must not serve as an end in itself, but as a means to an end. The goal is to inflame the heart. The mind is to serve as a feeding trough for the soul.

Consider the great teachers of church history. The titans include such figures as Saint Augustine, Saint

Thomas Aquinas, Martin Luther, John Calvin, and Jonathan Edwards. No more prodigious intellects have ever graced the theological scene than those of these men. Although each differs from the other in this or that point of theology, each man's writings reveal a soul in love with God. Theirs is no arid speculation, no academic detachment, no arrogant posture. They are men of passion who display a remarkable balance of the twin primacies of mind and heart.

Other theologians instruct, but few have been able to inspire as well. The giants of faith stir our hearts as they stimulate our minds. They have found rest for their souls and are able to communicate that rest to a restless church.

What we find in the lives and writings of the great saints is the elusive "something more" often promised by lesser preachers, but rarely found by casual seekers.

Is there really something more? Is there a level of Christian faith and devotion higher than the commonplace? Is there a state of the soul that involves more rest than restlessness?

The answer to all these questions is an emphatic *yes!*

In every generation there have been religious movements generated by a desire for something more and sustained by the promise to deliver this elusive "extra." Mysticism, Jansenism, Deeper Life, Holiness perfectionist movements, Abundant Life theology, charismatic theology, and a host of other movements have sought a simple method for making giant leaps into sanctification. Such movements die because of simplistic "methods" of quick and easy spiritual growth.

There are no quick and easy paths to spiritual maturity. The soul that seeks a deeper level of maturity must be prepared for a long, arduous task. If we are to seek the Kingdom of God, we must abandon any formulae that promise instant spiritual gratification.

Sometimes the quest for godliness resembles a spiritual recapitulation of Sisyphus, the mythical character condemned by the gods to the perpetual task of rolling a huge boulder to the summit of a treacherous slope. His "reward" for completing the task was to have the stone roll immediately back to the bottom of the hill, where he was obligated to begin the chore anew.

The frustrations of Sisyphus have counterparts in the physical realm we inhabit. I carry a card in my wallet that says, "Weight Watchers Lifetime Member." To earn such a card one must endure a dieting regimen that culminates in the attainment of a clearly defined weight goal that is maintained for a minimum of six weeks.

My hard-earned card mocks me. It reminds me of the time I lost forty-three pounds in sixteen weeks. The experience was exhilarating. Attending Weight Watchers meetings was similar to going to church or a Bible study. There were inspirational speeches, encouragement from the "brothers and sisters," and the ritual of weighing in and having your accomplishments recorded in an ominous booklet. One obese woman lost seventeen pounds the first week. When her achievement was announced to the group, she was moved to tears by the spontaneous standing ovation. Three weeks later, however, she dropped out of the program, apparently resigned to continued obesity.

But I hung in the program and reached my goal. No longer was I embarrassed to see my reflection in store windows. Nor was I ashamed to look at my body in a mirror. My wife bought me my first tailor-made suit. I had all my other suits and sport coats altered. My golf swing no longer had to make a detour around my stomach.

I memorized the Weight Watchers' "Bible verses": "Inch by inch it's a cinch;" "Nothing tastes as good as thin feels;" "We'll see less of you next week!"

Alas, three years have passed, and I have become

a Weight Watchers apostate. I've regained thirty of the pounds I labored so hard to lose. I avoid mirrors. I have one suit that fits. My golf swing has to be routed around my belly again. I am the Sisyphus of dieting. The thought of losing even ten pounds now seems like mission impossible.

My weight-loss experience shows me that a sustained effort over a short period of time can bring dramatic results. But for long-lasting, indeed permanent, results the effort must be sustained without ceasing.

So it is with spiritual attainment. We can shed sinful habits and desires momentarily after a brief exhilarating experience. But without sustained spiritual discipline, moments of spiritual achievement give way to ongoing failure. Authentic spirituality remains elusive.

Jesus said it is good to be spiritually hungry: "Blessed are they which do hunger and thirst after righteousness: for they shall be filled." Our physical lives oscillate between periods of hunger and times of feeding and fullness. When the stomach is full, we feel as if we'll never need to eat again. But as soon as the stomach is empty, the temptation to binge sets in.

Food that is permanent would allow us to escape the endless pattern of hunger, satiation, and hunger again. We need the bread of life for permanent satisfaction.

This metaphor of food and drink appears elsewhere in the teaching of Jesus, such as in his encounter with the Samaritan woman:

"There cometh a woman of Samaria to draw water: Jesus saith unto her, Give me to drink. (For his disciples were gone away unto the city to buy meat.) Then saith the woman of Samaria unto him, How is it that thou, being a Jew, askest drink of me, which am a woman of Samaria? for the Jews have no dealings with the Samaritans.

"Jesus answered and said unto her, If thou knewest the gift of God, and who it is that saith to thee, Give me to drink; thou wouldest have asked of him, and he would have given thee living water.

"The woman saith unto him, Sir, thou hast nothing to draw with, and the well is deep: from whence then hast thou that living water? Art thou greater than our father Jacob, which gave us the well, and drank thereof himself, and his children, and his cattle?

"Jesus answered and said unto her, Whosoever drinketh of this water shall thirst again: But whosoever drinketh of the water that I shall give him shall never thirst; but the water that I shall give him shall be in him a well of water springing up into everlasting life.

"The woman saith unto him, Sir, give me this water, that I thirst not, neither come hither to draw." (John 4:7-15)

One of the memories I savor from my first trip to the Holy Land is my visit to Samaria. Standing at the base of the mountain called Gerizim by the traditional site of Jacob's well, I contemplated the history that had converged there. The well, dug millennia ago, still functions. Its water assuages the thirst of modern seminomads even as it quenched the thirst of Jacob and his family.

Standing at the very spot where Jesus conversed with the woman of Sychar, I imagined hearing his voice, as if the sound waves remained suspended in time. The conversation started innocently as Jesus made a simple request: "Give me to drink."

In this ordinary plea resided a paradox of immense proportions. The Living Water was thirsty. The Creator of all water was now, in his incarnation, in need of water. Though his divine nature required no such physical sustenance, his human nature could not survive without it.

Before responding to Jesus' request, the woman interrogated him about his violation of the cultural taboo that Jews were to have no discourse with Samaritans.

Jesus seized the opportunity to provide a thinly veiled introduction of his true identity and gently chided her for not asking him for the water he alone could provide.

"If thou knewest the gift of God, and who it is that saith to thee, Give me to drink; thou wouldest have asked of him, and he would have given thee living water." (John 4:10)

The problem was that the woman did not know with whom she was speaking, and her ignorance could have caused her to lose the opportunity of a lifetime. The Author of rest held the cure to the woman's restlessness, but at the moment she knew it not.

I mention this obvious factor because it points beyond this isolated moment in history toward a perpetual human condition suffered by millions. Ignorance of the source of rest is the chief impediment to the possession of rest. As long as we remain uninformed regarding the source of rest, we are doomed to an abiding restlessness.

The woman was intrigued by the mention of living water, but skeptical. She pointed to two obstacles that seemingly made Jesus' offer impossible to deliver:

"Sir, thou hast nothing to draw with, and the well is deep." (John 4:11)

That Jesus stood there without an implement to draw water suggested to the woman that his boast was an idle one. He apparently lacked the means to carry out his offer. And the woman, at this point, lacked the faith necessary to receive the offer. The author of Hebrews declares:

"But without faith it is impossible to please him: for he that cometh to God must believe that he is, and that he is a rewarder of them that diligently seek him." (Hebrews 11:6)

This text introduces the famous "roll call" of the saints, a list of personages from the Old Testament who did believe that God is able to reward those who diligently seek him.

The woman of Sychar had not yet exhibited the faith of Noah, Abraham, Isaac, Jacob, Joseph, and the others. The irony is that it was possible for Jesus to give living water even though he had no pot with which to draw it and in spite of the depth of the well. But it was not possible for the woman to receive living water without faith in the one offering it. The woman raised a second question:

"Art thou greater than our father Jacob, which gave us the well . . . ?" (John 4:12)

Jesus was greater than Jacob, infinitely greater. He was Jacob's Creator and Redeemer. He was Jacob's ladder who bridged the chasm between heaven and earth, and upon whom angels ascended and descended. Ignoring the woman's question with its implied ridicule, Jesus pressed the point of his original offer:

"Whosoever drinketh of this water shall thirst again: but whosoever drinketh of the water that I shall give him shall never thirst; but the water that I shall give him shall be in him a well of water springing up into everlasting life." (John 4:13-14)

Water from Jacob's well could assuage the woman's thirst only temporarily. Jesus was speaking of a different sort of water—water that required neither bucket nor ladle to acquire, water that flowed from a completely new well. This well was not located on the edge of town, requiring a daily trek to fetch water from it. This well would be located within the woman herself, and its source would never run dry. This was water for the soul, not for the body.

Anyone who can give water to a dry, thirsty soul is greater than Jacob. This water is a reservoir that gushes into eternity.

Finally, the woman responded in faith: "Sir, give me this water" (John 4:15).

Hers is the request of every Christian. Give me that water, the water that wells up forever, forever bringing satisfaction to my soul.

To the thirsty woman of Sychar, Jesus revealed that he was the Messiah of Israel. She received that revelation and bore testimony to it:

"The woman then left her waterpot, and went her way into the city, and saith to the men, Come, see a man, which told me all things that ever I did: is not this the Christ?" (John 4:28-29)

The final irony in this episode is that the very implement that triggered the woman's skepticism—her waterpot—was left behind as she turned her attention from the water she had come to draw to meet her physical needs to the water she found to satisfy her spiritual needs.

If we combine Jesus' metaphors of thirst, we see that in order to be freed of thirst, we must first be earnestly engaged in thirst. Those who are not hungry have no hope of ever being filled. Those who are not thirsty will never have a wellspring within their own souls.

David likened his thirst to that of an exhausted deer:

"As the hart panteth after the water brooks, so panteth my soul after thee, O God. My soul thirsteth for God, for the living God." (Psalm 42:1-2)

I have never witnessed a deer panting after water, but I have seen my two German shepherds panting for water after chasing a deer. Although the dogs were trained to respond instantly to my commands, no amount of shouting from me could deter them from their pursuit once they started chasing a deer. No dog can run as fast as a deer, however, so only after the deer stops running due to exhaustion can a dog actually catch one. My shepherds always ran out of steam long before the deer. They would give up after two or three minutes.

When my dogs returned after a chase their tongues would be hanging out of their mouths, and they would be panting heavily, saliva dripping from their lips. They wanted water—desperately. They headed for the pond and lapped noisily. Somewhere in the woods I knew a deer was panting for water as well. Somewhere a deer's heart was racing after the chase.

David spent more time in the wild than I ever did, and I'm sure he saw what I only imagined. He saw the deer after it escaped its predator. He lived in a land where water was less plentiful than in Pennsylvania, and the heat more scorching.

A deer in such a condition has but one consuming passion—to quench its fierce thirst. It is that monomaniacal passion that David likened to his own soul's desire for God.

"My soul thirsteth for God, for the living God." (Psalm 42:2)

David's quest for something more was not a casual interest. It was no hobby. His motivation was not duty; it was desire. Need, not obligation, impelled his spirit.

A regimen of water drinking is often prescribed for people trying to lose weight. When drinking for this reason, the sight of one more full glass can be loathsome. When no thirst is present, it is difficult to drink. But it is easy to drink water when thirst demands to be quenched.

Jesus promised to fill those who hunger and thirst after righteousness. He made no promise to fill those who are not hungry.

2

SWEETNESS AND HONEY: LOVING THE WORD OF GOD

*T*HE SOUL IS AWAKENED TO GOD chiefly by the Spirit of God as he pierces our souls with the Word of God. At times we not only neglect that Word but flee from it as something sour and distasteful to us. Sometimes we view it as a revelatory smorgasbord from which we choose those portions that seem tasty to us while passing by the offerings we dislike.

In the life of the prophet Ezekiel, we meet an Old Testament saint who feasted upon the whole counsel of God. Even those words that were "hard sayings" became delectable to him. For Christians to progress in sanctification, they must develop an appetite for all of the Word of God—like Ezekiel.

The prophet Ezekiel was a victim of the Babylonian captivity. He was deported from his homeland and carried off to an alien and pagan nation. By the river Kebar he experienced a remarkable vision of the glory of God:

> "And I looked, and, behold, a whirlwind came out of the north, a great cloud, and a fire infolding itself, and a brightness was about it, and out of the midst thereof as the colour of amber, out of the midst of the fire." (Ezekiel 1:4)

The whirlwind, cloud, and fire indicate a kind of theophany. A theophany is an outward, visible manifestation of the invisible God, such as Moses saw in the burning bush and such as the Israelites followed through the wilderness in the form of a pillar of cloud and pillar of fire. Such visions usually involved some manifestation of fire and/or the appearance of the glory cloud called the shekinah, which is characterized by a radiant, dazzling brightness.

Such manifestations of divine glory always filled the beholder with dread and awe. It meant the terrifying presence of the living God, who is an all-consuming fire. Ezekiel's vision resembles the vision of the prophet Isaiah and that of John in the Apocalypse. However, what follows is unique to Ezekiel's vision:

> "Also out of the midst thereof came the likeness of four living creatures. And this was their appearance; they had the likeness of a man. And every one

had four faces, and every one had four wings. And their feet were straight feet; and the sole of their feet was like the sole of a calf's foot: and they sparkled like the colour of burnished brass." (Ezekiel 1:5-7)

The description of these four creatures calls to mind the cherubim God placed at the east of the Garden of Eden armed with a flaming sword to guard the tree of life (Genesis 3:24). They also resemble the four beasts that are around the throne by the sea of glass in Revelation 4:6-8, except that the creatures in John's vision had six wings, as did the seraphim in Isaiah 6.

The strange motion displayed by the creatures in Ezekiel has provoked all sorts of bizarre speculation, including the idea that Ezekiel was witnessing an ancient visitation by an alien in a flying saucer.

But the origin of the four living creatures was not Mars or Venus. Their abode was heaven itself. Ezekiel describes further:

"And they had the hands of a man under their wings on their four sides; and they four had their faces and their wings. Their wings were joined one to another; they turned not when they went; they went every one straight forward.

"As for the likeness of their faces, they four had the face of a man, and the face of a lion, on the right side: and they four had the face of an ox on the left side; they four also had the face of an eagle." (Ezekiel 1:8-10)

The four living creatures supported the platform for God's throne. They had a quasi-human form and stood upright. They had a human face and human hands, yet they differed dramatically from normal human beings. Each had four faces, four wings, and feet whose soles were like those of calves.

The four-faced creatures represented the highest forms of created life: man, mentioned first, faced forward; the lion was considered the king of the wild beasts; the ox was king of the domesticated animals; and the eagle was ruler of the sky.[1] These four-faced creatures appear again in Revelation 4:7. The faces were later used as symbols for the four gospel writers—Matthew was depicted in Christian art as a man, Mark as a lion, Luke as an ox, and John as an eagle.

The four creatures formed a perfect square. "Four-square" indicates perfect symmetry. No matter from which direction one observed the creatures, a different face was seen on all of them. All four faces were visible from any angle. The closest face would always be the human one; the face on the left would be the ox; the face on the right would be the lion; and the one in the rear would be the eagle.[2]

"Thus were their faces: and their wings were stretched upward; two wings of every one were joined one to another, and two covered their bodies." (Ezekiel 1:11)

The creatures were linked together by their wingtips. Two wings of each creature stretched out to touch the others, resembling the outspread wings of the cherubim who guarded the sacred ark of the covenant (see Exodus 25:20).

The creatures had only four wings, differing from the six-winged seraphim of Isaiah 6. Why only four wings? Presumably they had no need for the third pair, which were used for flight. These angelic creatures had a different form of locomotion. Two wings shielded their bodies from the divine glory, while the other two supported the heavenly platform on which God's throne stood.

"And they went every one straight forward: whither the spirit was to go, they went; and they turned not when they went. As for the likeness of the living creatures, their appearance was like burning coals of fire, and like the appearance of lamps: it went up and down among the living creatures; and the fire was bright, and out of the fire went forth lightning. And the living creatures ran and returned as the appearance of a flash of lightning." (Ezekiel 1:12-14)

Though scholars disagree about the meaning of this portion of the vision, I believe it conveys the idea of motion impelled by the divine Spirit. In a commentary on Ezekiel, Walter Eichrodt observes:

> What is envisaged is not progress along the surface of the earth, but hovering among the clouds, which form the brightly shining background against which the figures are seen. They have no will of their own, but are ruled by the might of the Spirit streaming through them. Because they face to all four points of the compass, it is unnecessary for them to turn, and thus they always appear as if seen from the front.[3]

In the center of the hollow square made by the four living creatures was the bright fire, the burning coals and lamps, punctuated by flashes of lightning. These images all suggest theophany. In Abraham's vision in which God swore an oath by himself, God appeared as a smoking furnace and burning lamp that moved between the pieces of carved animals (Genesis 15:17), clearly indicating the divine presence. As the lightning of God flashed on Mt. Sinai, here it signaled the movement of the angelic beings propelled by the Holy Spirit of God.

EZEKIEL'S WHEELS

The following part of the prophet's vision describes the heavenly chariot-throne of God, a chariot of fire symbolizing God's glorious presence:

"Now as I beheld the living creatures, behold one wheel upon the earth by the living creatures, with his four faces. The appearance of the wheels and their work was like unto the colour of a beryl: and they four had one likeness: and their appearance and their work was as it were a wheel in the middle of a wheel.

"When they went, they went upon their four sides: and they turned not when they went. As for their rings, they were so high that they were dreadful; and their rings were full of eyes round about them four. And when the living creatures went, the wheels went by them: and when the living creatures were lifted up from the earth, the wheels were lifted up. Whithersoever the spirit was to go, they went, thither was their spirit to go; and the wheels were lifted up over against them: for the spirit of the living creature was in the wheels.

"When those went, these went; and when those stood, these stood; and when those were lifted up from the earth, the wheels were lifted up over against them: for the spirit of the living creature was in the wheels." (Ezekiel 1:15-21)

This vision is almost, if not altogether, impossible for us to imagine. The text suggests an object that had wheels consisting of two discs that bisected each other at right angles. They were able to move in any direction without being turned. That they were "full of eyes" made them a terrifying sight. The vision suggests a divine chariot-throne that stands over and above this world. The wheels within wheels indicate God's omnipresence. The chariot can easily lift itself from the earth and fly in any direction. It is neither fixed nor bound.[4]

The glory-chariot of God appears elsewhere in Scripture. Elijah departed this earth in a chariot of fire:

"And it came to pass, as they still went on, and talked, that, behold, there appeared a chariot of fire, and horses of fire, and parted them both asunder; and Elijah went up by a whirlwind into heaven." (2 Kings 2:11)

This extraordinary sight was witnessed by Elijah's disciple, Elisha, and it was not to be Elisha's last view of divine things that stand behind the veil. To ambush Elisha, the king of Syria dispatched a large military expedition of soldiers, horses, and chariots to surround Dothan at night. When Elisha's servant arose in the morning, he was terrified to see that they were surrounded by the Syrian horde. He roused Elisha and warned him of their peril. Elisha, remaining calm, said:

"Fear not: for they that be with us are more than they that be with them.

"And Elisha prayed, and said, LORD, I pray thee, open his eyes, that he may see. And the LORD opened the eyes of the young man; and he saw: and, behold, the mountain was full of horses and chariots of fire round about Elisha." (2 Kings 6:16-17)

God enabled Elisha to see beyond the normal scope of human perception into another dimension. What was invisible was made visible to him.

Beyond the record of sacred Scripture there is at least one dramatic historical record of the vision of the divine chariots. It comes from the Jewish historian Josephus, who provided a detailed account and eyewitness report of the siege of Jerusalem by the Roman armies under the leadership of

Titus. Josephus gives his account with some trepidation, obviously fearful that the report would be too extraordinary for any sober reader to believe:

> Then again, not many days after the feast, on the twenty-first of the month of Artemisium, a supernatural apparition was seen, too amazing to be believed. What I am now to relate would, I imagine, have been dismissed as imaginary, had this not been vouched for by eyewitnesses, then followed by subsequent disasters that deserved to be thus signalized. For before sunset chariots were seen in the air over the whole country, and armed battalions speeding through the clouds and encircling the cities. Then again, at the feast called Pentecost, when the priests had entered the inner courts of the Temple by night to perform their usual ministrations, they declared that they were aware, at first, of a violent commotion and din, then of a voice as of a host crying, "We are departing hence."[5]

If this extraordinary record has any semblance to reality, it is striking that the heavenly chariots announced their departure just before the worst catastrophe ever to befall Zion. The divine chariots that protected Elisha ceased protecting Israel when God's judgment fell upon Jerusalem.

THE DIVINE GLORY

Ezekiel's vision reached its climax with the manifestation of divine glory:

"And the likeness of the firmament upon the heads of the living creature was as the colour of the terrible crystal, stretched forth over their heads above. And under the firmament were their wings straight, the one toward the other: every one had two, which covered on this side, and every one had two, which covered on that side, their bodies.

"And when they went, I heard the noise of their wings, like the noise of great waters, as the voice of the Almighty, the voice of speech, as the noise of an host: when they stood, they let down their wings. . . . And above the firmament that was over their heads was the likeness of a throne, as the appearance of a sapphire stone: and upon the likeness of the throne was the likeness as the appearance of a man above upon it.

"And I saw as the colour of amber, as the appearance of fire round about within it, from the appearance of his loins even upward, and from the appearance of his loins even downward, I saw as it were the appearance of fire, and it had brightness round about." (Ezekiel 1:22-27)

This vision anticipates the sea of glass in Revelation 4:6. Ezekiel sees a figure like a man seated upon a heavenly throne. The figure exudes a fiery presence, blazing with the brightness of divine majesty.

"As the appearance of the bow that is in the cloud in the day of rain, so was the appearance of the brightness round about. This was the appearance of the likeness of the glory of the LORD. And when I saw it, I fell upon my face, and I heard a voice of one that spake." (Ezekiel 1:28)

Ezekiel's view of the rainbow is mirrored in John's vision in Revelation 4:3. The refulgent glory that shone round about drove Ezekiel to the ground. He fell on his face, a standard biblical response of humans who behold the glory of God. It was probably the posture of Isaiah at his call (Isaiah 6) and certainly that of Peter, James, and John at the Mount of Transfiguration (Matthew 17:6).

While Ezekiel was prostrate God spoke to him. He did not hear the voice of God until he was flat on his face before him.

"And he said unto me, Son of man, stand upon thy feet, and I will speak unto thee. And the spirit entered into me when he spake unto me, and set me upon my feet, that I heard him that spake unto me." (Ezekiel 2:1-2)

In this moment, God did two things to the prophet. First, he sent his Spirit *into* him. Second, he set him on his feet. Ezekiel did not rise by his own power. His impotence before the majesty of God was healed by the power of the Spirit of God. The sequence is important. First he is indwelt by the Spirit, then he is able to stand and to hear the word of God.

THE PROPHETIC CALL AND COMMISSION

The Old Testament prophets did not receive their credentials from human institutions. They did not belong to an ordinary line of servants, such as those who inherited their positions as Levitical priests. To qualify for the role of prophet, one had to receive a direct and immediate call from God, even as New Testament apostles were authorized by a direct commission from Christ. The prophet, like the apostle, is one sent on a mission by God to speak the word of God with nothing less than divine authority. In Israel the prophets served as God's prosecuting attorneys. Armed with divine subpoenas, they were to file suit against Israel for breaking their covenant with God.

In chapter 2, Ezekiel records the content of his call, that which will define his vocation:

"And he said unto me, Son of man, I send thee to the children of Israel, to a rebellious nation that hath rebelled against me: they and their fathers have transgressed against me, even unto this very day. For they are impudent children and stiffhearted. I do send thee unto them; and thou shalt say unto them, Thus saith the Lord GOD.

"And they, whether they will hear, or whether they will forbear, (for they are a rebellious house,) yet shall know that there hath been a prophet among them." (Ezekiel 2:3-5)

Ezekiel is sent not to utter his own opinions nor to vent his own anger. He is commissioned to speak the message of God. He is to preface his message with "Thus saith the Lord God," not "This is what I think." Here we see an example of the dual source of the authorship of sacred Scripture. Though the text of the Bible is written by human authors, it is nevertheless the *vox Dei*, the voice of God. The writers are the messengers, but the message is God's.

FEAR TO BE OVERCOME

The prophetic task was onerous to all who bore it. Which of the prophets was not hated and persecuted by his own people? There was much, humanly speaking, to fear. The chief requisite for the prophet was courage:

"And thou, son of man, be not afraid of them, neither be afraid of their words, though briers and thorns be with thee, and thou dost dwell among scorpions: be not afraid of their words, nor be dismayed at their looks, though they be a rebellious house. And thou shalt speak my words unto them, whether they will hear, or whether they will forbear: for they are most rebellious." (Ezekiel 2:6-7)

The images God uses in his admonition to the prophet are graphic. He is sending Ezekiel to a place surrounded by thorns and briers. This may be a good haven for Br'er Rabbit, but it is a desolate and threatening habitat for human beings. Unlike Eden, where no thorn or brier grew, thorns and briers indicate the place where God's curse is found. It is a place inhabited by scorpions, similar to the wilderness of Judea, where Jesus was exposed to the assault of Satan for forty days.

In this house of desolation Ezekiel will be exposed to angry words and hostile glances. He will have to endure insults, slander, and endless criticism, things that easily intimidate many preachers. Every preacher acquires the skill of reading the body language of his congregation. He can read their faces and know when they are bored or angry. One hostile look may be all it takes to make a preacher change his message in midsentence to accommodate the wishes of his hearers. This skill, born of fear and intimidation, was mastered by the false prophets of Israel. It was prohibited to Ezekiel:

"But thou, son of man, hear what I say unto thee; Be not thou rebellious like that rebellious house: open thy mouth, and eat that I give thee." (Ezekiel 2:8)

Ezekiel is called to be different. Though he is an Israelite, a member of the rebellious house, he is not to participate in their rebellion.

God does not hold Ezekiel responsible for making the people listen to God's word. His responsibilities are, first, to hear the word of God even if no one else is willing to listen to it, and second, to proclaim it with full fidelity.

Ezekiel's task echoes that of another prophet, who remained behind in Israel. What Ezekiel was to prophesy from captivity, Jeremiah was called to proclaim at home. The same responsibility was given to both men.

When Jeremiah complained that the people preferred the message of the false prophets to his own, God replied:

"I have heard what the prophets said, that prophesy lies in my name, saying, I have dreamed, I have dreamed. How long shall this be in the heart of the prophets that prophesy lies? yea, they are prophets of the deceit of their own heart; which think to cause my people to forget my name by their dreams, which they tell every man to his neighbour, as their fathers have forgotten my name for Baal.

"The prophet that hath a dream, let him tell a dream; and he that hath my word, let him speak my word faithfully. What is the chaff to the wheat? saith the LORD." (Jeremiah 23:25-28)

Like Jeremiah, Ezekiel was called to be "wheat," eschewing the habits of the "chaff." His job was not to worry about what others said or did. His task was to be faithful to the word he received from God.

To ensure that Ezekiel fully embraced the commissioned word, God commanded him to eat it:

"And when I looked, behold, an hand was sent unto me; and, lo, a roll of a book was therein; And he spread it before me; and it was written within and without: and there was written therein lamentations, and mourning, and woe. Moreover he said unto me, Son of man, eat that thou findest; eat this roll, and go speak unto the house of Israel." (Ezekiel 2:9–3:1)

God commanded Ezekiel to consume the scroll. Its message was hardly good news. It was not the gospel he was told to devour. This food of God's word was one of lamentations, mourning, and woe. It was an oracle of divine judgment and wrath. It was a diet of bitterness.

A parallel command was given to John in Revelation 10:9-10:

"And I went unto the angel, and said unto him, Give me the little book. And he said unto me, Take it, and eat it up; and it shall make thy belly bitter, but it shall be in thy mouth sweet as honey. And I took the little book out of the angel's hand, and ate it up; and it was in my mouth sweet as honey: and as soon as I had eaten it, my belly was bitter."

Ezekiel's experience was the same:

"So I opened my mouth, and he caused me to eat that roll. And he said unto me, Son of man, cause thy belly to eat, and fill thy bowels with this roll that I give thee. Then did I eat it; and it was in my mouth as honey for sweetness. And he said unto me, Son of man, go, get thee unto the house of Israel, and speak with my words unto them." (Ezekiel 3:2-4)

God commanded Ezekiel to do more than chew and swallow the scroll. He told him to fill his bowels with it. It was not enough to taste the word of God; he was to digest it. God demanded that his word fill Ezekiel's bloodstream, that it become a visceral part of him.

Ezekiel experienced "something more." His personal religious experience transcended that of the normal Christian life. God does not give us today visible displays of divine glory as he gave to Ezekiel. But we do have the Word of God. Indeed we possess God's Word in fuller measure than even Ezekiel enjoyed.

We have the gospel to taste, chew on, swallow, and digest. It leaves no bitterness in our bellies. Yet something inhibits our taste buds. When we read portions of Scripture that reveal lamentations, mourning, and woe, they seldom taste to us as sweetness and honey.

Why did such words taste so sweet to Ezekiel? Certainly not because he had a sadistic spirit or because he was so hostile to his own people that he delighted in hearing of God's judgment upon them.

No, Ezekiel could taste sweetness and honey for two reasons. The first is related to the remarkable vision he saw. Once he saw the visible manifestation of God's glory he was captured, heart and soul, by an understanding of the holiness of God. To find the elusive "something more," every one of us must first be captivated by the holiness of God. Only a view of divine holiness can drive a Christian to become a human reflection of that holiness.

Second, the hard sayings of God were sweetness and honey to Ezekiel because he understood that even God's wrath and judgment are an expression of his purity.

The Christian who seeks a deeper experience of God by ignoring the hard sayings of Scripture gets nowhere. The full nourishment of the soul requires feeding on the whole counsel of God.

Ezekiel experienced more than revelation. Added to the revelation was the supernatural gift of illumination. Only when Scripture is illumined by the

Holy Spirit does it become, in its entirety, sweetness and honey. It is this illumination that we must seek and discover if we are to experience the sweetness of the Word of God.

3

DIVINE ILLUMINATION: THE SECRET OF CHRISTIAN PROGRESS

*C*HRISTIAN HISTORY REVEALS AN EBB and flow of divine visitations of grace by which large numbers of people were awakened to a deeper level in the holy pursuit of God. Certain movements in history stand out as moments of extraordinary awakening. In the eighteenth century, America experienced what historians call the Great Awakening. The Great Awakening was fueled in large measure by the influence of the great English Puritans who left a legacy in New England.

If any group of Christians ever exemplified the Christian life it was the Puritans, who were vigorous in their pursuit of personal holiness. None exceeded the level attained by America's greatest theologian, Puritan Jonathan Edwards. If any man ever understood the secret to finding something more, to finding rest for the soul, it was Edwards.

In 1734 Edwards preached a sermon in North-ampton, Massachusetts, that was soon after publish-ed at the urging of his congregation. This sermon is far less known than his "Sinners in the Hands of an Angry God," which he preached in Enfield seven years later, but the earlier sermon is crucial for our understanding of the "secret" to progress in the Christian life.

The title of the 1734 sermon was "A Divine and Supernatural Light, Immediately Imparted to the Soul by the Spirit of God, Shown to Be Both a Scriptural and Rational Doctrine."

The title itself is enough to intimidate modern readers. The text of the sermon was Matthew 16:17:

"And Jesus answered and said unto him, Blessed art thou, Simon Bar-jona: for flesh and blood hath not revealed it unto thee, but my Father which is in heaven."

The text was drawn from the discourse contain-ing Peter's "Great Confession" at Caesarea Philippi, where Jesus inquired of his disciples concerning popular views of his identity. He first asked them, "Whom do men say that I, the Son of Man, am?"

After hearing the public consensus, Jesus then asked the disciples: "But whom say ye that I am?"

Peter declared emphatically, "Thou art the Christ, the Son of the living God."

In response to this confession Jesus said, "Blessed art thou. . . ." Edwards explains this by saying:

> Thou art distinguishly happy. Others are blinded, and have dark and deluded apprehensions, as you have now given an account, some thinking that I am Elias, and some that I am Jeremias, and some one thing, and some another; but none of them thinking right, all of them misled. Happy art thou, that art so distinguished as to know the truth in this matter.[1]

The first thing we notice here is that the blessedness, the singular felicity enjoyed by Simon Peter, was related to a peculiar understanding of truth. Contrary to the popular maxim "Ignorance is bliss," Peter's bliss was rooted in correct knowledge.

The modern Christian tends to ignore or decry the importance of right doctrine. Tired of endless disputes, Christians today embrace the idea that what really matters is right relationships, not right doctrine. The idea that one is more important than the other is a faulty premise; both right relationships and right doctrine matter. Furthermore, to say that relationships hold more value than doctrine is an arrogant attitude that violates the character of the Holy Spirit, who is the Spirit of truth. The Christian who is careless with truth is, at best, far from the blessedness of which Peter partook and, at worst, no Christian at all.

Edwards understood, however, that correct knowledge, abstractly considered, was not enough. It is a particular kind of knowledge grasped in a particular way that is crucial to blessedness.

The foundation of Peter's blessedness was a knowledge not gained by natural means (i.e., by "flesh and blood").

Edwards believed, as did Augustine, and Aquinas before him, that "God is the author of all knowledge and understanding whatsoever. He is the author of all moral prudence, and of the skill that men have in their secular business."[2]

Edwards means more than that God created human beings with a brain and the skill to learn things on their own via rational speculation or empirical investigation. That God is the *author* of all knowledge means that he, himself, is the *source* of such knowledge. All knowledge rests on the revelation of God. This revelation refers not only to the special revelation given in Scripture but also to the general revelation God gives in nature.

Saint Augustine argued that just as the eye is

dependent upon light to be able to see anything (the human eye perceives nothing in total darkness), so there can be no knowledge of anything without the prior light of divine revelation.[3]

The knowledge that produces blessedness is knowledge given by special revelation. It is more than can be gleaned from the light of nature. In describing secular, or natural, knowledge Edwards says:

> God is the author of such knowledge; yet so that flesh and blood reveals it. Mortal men are capable of imparting the knowledge of human arts and sciences, and skill in temporal affairs. God is the author of such knowledge by those means: flesh and blood is employed as the *mediate*, or *second*, cause of it: he conveys it by the power and influence of natural means.[4]

Edwards then distinguishes between secular knowledge and the knowledge given to Peter at Caesarea Philippi:

> But this spiritual knowledge spoken of in the text, is what God is the author of, and none else. He imparts this knowledge immediately, not making use of any intermediate natural causes, as he does in other knowledge.[5]

Edwards uses language here that his congregation was well familiar with, but that is not common to modern Christians.

The distinction Edwards makes is between revelation *immediately* communicated by God and revelation that is *mediately* communicated. Used in ordinary speech, the word *immediately* refers to something that happens "right now." Using it in a more technical sense, however, Edwards means "without any intermediate causes." Immediate revelation comes directly from God to the receiver. No object, book, person, or any other thing acts as a conveyor of the message. It comes directly from the mind of God to the mind of man.

In the rest of his sermon, Edwards enlarges on the nature of this divine light and how it is obtained.

To give clear definition to the divine and supernatural light he begins by using negation. That is, he first says what it is not:

> Those convictions that natural men may have of their sin and misery, is not this spiritual and divine light. Men in a natural condition may have convictions of the guilt that lies upon them, and of the anger of God, and their danger of divine vengeance. Such convictions are from the light of truth. . . . Conscience is a principle

natural to men; and the work that it doth naturally, or of itself, is to give an apprehension of right and wrong. . . . But in the renewing and sanctifying work of the Holy Ghost, those things are wrought in the soul that are above nature, and of which there is nothing of the like kind in the soul by nature. . . .[6]

Here we approach the essence of Edwards's teaching, where he talks about a knowledge that gets beyond the mind and pierces the soul. We can understand a doctrine with our mind. We may even have a perfectly orthodox understanding of the truth without that truth ever piercing our soul. It is the soul-piercing understanding that we are after, the understanding wrought within us by the Holy Spirit.

My first personal experience of this sort of thing happened the night I was converted. I was led to Christ by a football player in the freshman dorm at college. In our conversation he mentioned none of the classic "salvation" texts. Instead, he discussed the book of Ecclesiastes with me. One verse hit me between the eyes, gripped my soul, and wrenched me from my dogmatic slumber:

"If the clouds be full of rain, they empty themselves upon the earth: and if the tree fall toward the south, or toward the north, in the place where the tree falleth, there it shall be." (Ecclesiastes 11:3)

What could be more obvious than the idea that "where a tree falls, there it lies"? But to me this simple concept was profound because I saw myself as a tree about to topple over. Indeed I had already toppled over, and unless something happened I was going to lie there and rot. I was unable to dial 911 and cry, "I've fallen, and I can't get up!" Instantly I knew I needed far more help than I could ever summon by telephone. It was this image that drove me to my knees in repentance. The Holy Spirit gave me no new revelation. Ecclesiastes 11:3 had been in print for millennia. But it struck my soul. This striking was not revelation; it was divine illumination by which the original revelation was directly applied to me. I often wonder if any other person has been converted by this text.

Edwards further distinguishes between how the Holy Spirit acts toward the unbeliever and how he acts toward the believer:

> He may indeed act upon the mind of a natural man, but he acts on the mind of a saint as an indwelling vital principle. He acts upon the mind of an unregenerate person as an extrinsic

occasional agent; for in acting upon them, he doth not unite himself to them; for notwithstanding all his influences that they may possess, they are still sensual, having not the Spirit.[7]

Edwards is describing a non-Christian, not a carnal Christian. Edwards knew nothing of so-called carnal Christians and would probably regard the concept as a contradiction in terms. Unregenerate people may experience the Holy Spirit acting *upon* them. What they lack is the Holy Spirit dwelling and acting *within* them.

But he unites himself with the mind of a saint, takes him as a new supernatural principle of life and action. There is this difference, that the Spirit of God, in acting in the soul of a godly man, exerts and communicates himself there in his own proper nature. Holiness is the proper nature of the Spirit of God.[8]

Edwards is careful to distinguish the illumination of the Holy Spirit from new revelation. This is a point of contention in our day between traditional Christians and those who embrace forms of neo-Pentecostal theology. Many today, including television preachers Benny Hinn and Robert

Tilton, claim that they receive new, private revelations from God. Edwards would urge us to run for our lives from such preachers:

> This spiritual light is not the suggesting of any new truths or propositions not contained in the Word of God. This suggesting of new truths or doctrines to the mind, independent of any antecedent revelation of those propositions, either in word or writing, is inspiration; such as the prophets and apostles had, and such as some enthusiasts pretend to. But this spiritual light that I am speaking of, is quite a different thing from inspiration. It reveals no new doctrine, it suggests no new proposition to the mind, it teaches no new thing of God, or Christ, or another world, not taught in the Bible, but only gives a due apprehension of those things that are taught in the Word of God.[9]

The key to this paragraph is found in the last phrase: *gives a due apprehension*. The Holy Spirit originally inspired the biblical revelation. Illumination of that revelation is a distinctly different work of the Holy Spirit. The Spirit assists us in understanding the text in a manner that is due the Word of God. This is the *due apprehension* of which Edwards speaks.

Edwards indicates that non-Christians can be affected to some degree by religious matters or even by reading the Bible. But these effects fall far short of what he is describing.

When I was a boy my parents made me go to church. I hated it. I found the whole affair insufferably boring. The hour from eleven to twelve o'clock on Sunday morning was the week's longest and most tedious. The only time I enjoyed going to church was on Christmas Eve because I loved the Christmas carols and the choral anthems. I had some appreciation for the spirit of Christmas, but it was that of a pagan.

The first Christmas Eve service after my conversion was unforgettable. My soul was enraptured, and all previous enjoyment was eclipsed by the glorious delight I now knew. Every carol took on new meaning. The words of the hymns were sweetness to me. It was a spiritual feast to truly celebrate for the first time the advent of the Savior.

THE POSITIVE NATURE OF THE SUPERNATURAL LIGHT

After describing what spiritual light is not, Edwards defines precisely what it is:

And it may be thus described: A true sense of the divine excellency of the things revealed in the Word of God, and a conviction of the truth and reality of them thence arising. This spiritual light primarily consists in the former of these, viz., a real sense and apprehension of the divine excellency of the things revealed in the Word of God. A spiritual and saving conviction of the truth and reality of these things, arises from such a sight of their divine excellency and glory; so that this conviction of their truth is an effect and natural consequence of this sight of their divine glory.[10]

Here Edwards stresses that although the divine and supernatural light *includes* a conviction of the truth of Scripture, this is not its primary effect. The primary effect is the *sense of divine excellency* of the truth of God. Edwards adds:

There is a divine and superlative glory in these things; an excellency that is of a vastly higher land, and more sublime nature, than in other things; a glory greatly distinguishing them from all that is earthly and temporal. He that is spiritually enlightened truly apprehends and sees it, or has a sense of it. He does not merely rationally believe that God is glorious, but he has a sense of the gloriousness of God in his heart. There is not only a rational belief that God is holy, and that holiness is a good thing, but there is a sense of the loveliness of God's holiness . . . there is a difference between having an *opinion* that God is holy and gracious, and having a *sense* of the loveliness and beauty of that holiness and grace. There is a difference between having a rational judgment that honey is sweet, and having a sense of its sweetness.[11]

The intellect is intimately involved in the "sense" of which Edwards speaks, but, as he maintains, "The will, or inclination, or heart are mainly concerned."[12]

In college I majored in philosophy and continued that study as a minor in graduate school. The benefit of studying philosophy, I found, went beyond simply knowing the content of the great philosophies of history. It involved the development of a skill called critical analysis. At times, but not always, critical analysis may be a negative form of criticism. It involves a close analytical scrutiny of the soundness of arguments, the use or misuse of rational inferences, and the application of principles of logic, such as the laws of immediate inference.

After such study I developed a habit of reading

with a critical eye. By this I do not mean cynicism; I mean concentration and analysis. I want to *understand* what I read whether I agree with it or not.

When I read the Bible, I approach it differently from the way I approach other forms of literature. It is not that the critical apparatus in my mind shuts down. If anything, my penchant for analysis is accentuated and sharpened when I read Scripture because I am motivated by a profound desire to understand Scripture. I want to understand Immanuel Kant, but I am far more motivated to understand the Bible.

The difference is chiefly this: When I read Scripture I am never "critical" of it in the negative sense. Rather I discover that I am the object of criticism. When I read the Bible, the Bible criticizes me.

I have spent many years reading the technical writings of scholars who espouse all kinds of "higher criticism" approaches to the Bible. These scholars do not hesitate to offer severe negative judgments about the text of the Bible, as well as its message. What is conspicuously absent in such literature is any sense that those criticizing it grasp the divine excellency of the things they are criticizing.

I sometimes wonder what motivates these scholars. Perhaps they are driven by a desire to disprove the credibility of the Book that criticizes them so severely and calls them to repentance. It is as the Dutch phenomenologist Luijpen once said of Jean-Paul Sartre: "Sartre's morality makes the denial of God necessary."[13]

Yet I stand in awe at the prodigious labor the higher critics exhibit. They are painstaking in their research and at times extraordinary in their erudition. They repeatedly offer invaluable technical insights that aid us in better understanding the text. Is there no delight in their work?

Of course there is. Intellectual analysis of any literature can be exhilarating. Pedantic research can be great fun. I understand the thrill of discovering a rare nuance of a strange verb form. I love to play Trivial Pursuit. Choice morsels of detail stimulate the mind. To recall some obscure fact that most people overlook or have forgotten boosts the ego. How many people know that Stan Rojek, who played shortstop for the Pittsburgh Pirates in 1948, had a father who was a milkman?

Intellectual delight in academic or even trivial matters is a delight we enjoy by nature. It requires no divine and supernatural light of which Edwards spoke. But to delight in the loveliness of the Word of God requires assistance from above. It demands the transcendent and supernatural work of the Holy Spirit not only upon us, but within us.

The Scripture tells us that we are by nature at enmity with God. The natural man approaches Scripture with a built-in hostility. In a word, we come to the text with *prejudice*. Edwards says:

> The mind of man is naturally full of prejudices against divine truth. It is full of enmity against the doctrines of the Gospel; which is a disadvantage to those arguments that prove their truth, and causes them to lose their force upon the mind. But when a person has discovered to him the divine excellency of Christian doctrines, this destroys the enmity, removes those prejudices, sanctifies the reason, and causes it to lie open to the force of arguments for their truth.[14]

The illumination of the divine and supernatural light not only impresses the mind, but more importantly it changes the disposition of the heart. What was odious becomes a matter of delight. When Edwards speaks of a sanctified reason he is not describing some magical increase in IQ or heightening of mental capacity. Rather, he is describing a reason that has been liberated from a hostile prejudice that once clouded and obscured judgment.

At conversion the disposition of the human soul

is radically altered. The natural enmity toward the Word of God is conquered but not altogether destroyed. Throughout life Christians continue to struggle with a residual prejudice against elements of the Word of God. Our minds begin the process of sanctification, but they are not yet glorified.

A word of advice I often give my seminary students is this: As you study the Bible, take special care to mark the passages you find difficult to accept. That is, mark the passages you don't like. Then give special attention to them. Closer scrutiny may reveal that you simply failed to understand the meaning of the text. At the very least, the extra study will give you a new understanding of the Word of God.

But suppose that after further study you remain convinced that your understanding is correct, but you still don't like what it says. This is a golden opportunity for rapid advance in sanctification. If you don't like what the Bible says, there is either something wrong with the Word of God or something wrong with your thinking. By isolating these texts you have a quick and easy way of discovering where your thinking is out of sync with the mind of Christ. You know exactly where you need to repent or change your mind.

While in seminary I had a card on my desk that

read: You are required to believe, to teach, and to preach what the Bible says, not what you want it to say.

I consulted the card frequently, especially when I struggled with the doctrine of predestination. Over the years, a pattern developed. First I would be convinced of the truth of the biblical teaching I didn't like. Then I would see the sweetness of those truths so that I delighted in them rather than despised them.

HOW ILLUMINATION IS GIVEN

After finishing his definition of the divine and supernatural light, Edwards shows *how* it is given immediately by God. Though our natural faculties are actively involved in this reality, they are not the cause or source of it, Edwards says:

> Indeed a person cannot have spiritual light without the word. But that does not argue that the word properly causes that light. The mind cannot see the excellency of any doctrine, unless that doctrine be first in the mind; but seeing the excellency of the doctrine may be immediately from the Spirit of God; though the conveying of the doctrine or proposition itself may be by the word. So that the notions

which are the subject matter of this light, are conveyed to the mind by the word of God; but that due sense of the heart, wherein this light formally consists, is immediately by the Spirit of God.[15]

This paragraph is perhaps the most important in Edwards's treatment of the matter. To put his thoughts another way: The biblical revelation gets the Word of God to the mind. The immediate illumination of the Holy Spirit carries it from the mind to the heart.

The Word of God can be in the mind without being in the heart; but it cannot be in the heart without first being in the mind. This point is crucial to answer the question, What can I do to get the divine and supernatural light into my heart?

Since the divine and supernatural light of illumination is conveyed by the *immediate* operation of the Holy Spirit, there is no magical formula by which we can force it to happen. The operation of the Holy Spirit in this matter is not only immediate; it is also sovereign, as God is sovereign. The Spirit moves as he pleases, not as we demand.

Does that then mean there is nothing we can do to receive this light? By no means. There is much that we can and should do in pursuit of divine illumination.

The first thing we must do is get the Word of God into our minds. That responsibility is ours, not God's. We are required to be diligent in our study of Scripture. We cannot reasonably expect the Spirit to give us the excellent sense of the Scripture in our hearts if we are unwilling to work to get it in our minds. A cavalier approach to Scripture will not do. The only "devotional" reading of God's Word that pleases him is a devout *study* of his Word.

The church is plagued by the heresy of so-called spiritual or pneumatic exegesis by which Christians are urged to abandon all books except the Bible and to go into their prayer closets and simply ask the Holy Spirit to teach them directly. This method has spawned innumerable heresies, all slanderously assigned to the Holy Ghost as their author.

Divine illumination comes through grace, not magic. This grace aids and assists our earnest and diligent study of Scripture. Members of Edwards's congregation, who enjoyed firsthand experience of an awakening to spiritual light, regularly had their Greek New Testaments propped open before them as they plowed their fields.

To get the Word of God into our minds, we must avail ourselves of the teaching aids God has given to the church. He set teachers in the church because we are usually poor teachers of ourselves. So we consult the commentaries, do our lessons, and diligently seek to master the text of Scripture.

Knowing that such study is necessary and cannot be circumvented, we are also aware that it is not enough. It may get the Word into our minds, but we want more; we want it in our hearts.

For this we must entreat the Holy Spirit to grant us illumination. Though we cannot demand it of him, he invites us to request it, for God is pleased to grant such grace to those who humbly and diligently pursue it. He does not give stones to those who ask for bread.

Such illumination is the "secret" of the Christian life. When the Word of God gets beyond the mind and into the heart, then and only then do our lives really change. We pass from a consciousness of the Word of God to a conviction of it, and then to a conscience that delights in it. It is when we obey God out of inward delight that we please him.

Edwards concludes his sermon by saying:

> Yea, the least glimpse of the glory of God in the face of Christ doth more exalt and ennoble the soul, than all the knowledge of those that

have the greatest speculative understanding in divinity without grace. . . .

This knowledge is that which is above all others sweet and joyful. . . . This spiritual light is the dawning of the light of glory in the heart. There is nothing so powerful as this to support persons in affliction, and to give the mind peace and brightness in this stormy and dark world.[16]

Edwards marvels that spiritual light not only exalts and ennobles the soul, gives support and peace in affliction, and lends sweetness and joy to the Christian pilgrimage, but also produces real sanctification:

This light is such as effectually influences the inclination, and changes the nature of the soul. . . . This light, and this only, has its fruit in an universal holiness of life. No merely notional or speculative understanding of the doctrines of religion will ever bring to this. But this light, as it reaches the bottom of the heart, and changes the nature, so it will effectually dispose to an universal obedience. It shows God as worthy to be obeyed and served. It draws forth the heart in a sincere love to God, which is the only principle of a true, gracious, and universal obedience; and it convinces of the reality of those glorious rewards that God has promised to them that obey him.[17]

Obedience is the fruit of this marvelous operation of the Holy Spirit, who works in and through the Word. When the Spirit teaches us his Word, our hearts become inflamed.

4

THE WITNESS
OF THE
HOLY SPIRIT

*E*DWARDS'S TREATMENT OF THE divine and supernatural light is but an expansion of the important doctrine taught by John Calvin in the sixteenth century. Calvin developed the doctrine of the internal testimony of the Holy Spirit, which is a focal point of Reformation theology.

Concerning the question of the Bible's authority, Calvin strongly rejected the Roman Catholic teachings that the authority of Scripture rests in some manner on the authority of the church. He writes:

> A most pernicious error has very generally prevailed—viz. that Scripture is of importance only insofar as conceded to it by the suffrage of the Church; as if the eternal and unviolable truth of God could depend on the will of men.

With great insult to the Holy Spirit, it is asked,
Who can assure us that the Scriptures pro-
ceeded from God; who guarantee that they
have come down safe and unimpaired to our
times; who persuade us that this book is to be
received with reverence, and that one ex-
punged from the list, did not the church regu-
late all these things with certainty?[1]

It is important to note that Calvin is not speaking of
proof of the Bible's authority; he is speaking of the
persuasion (or assurance) of that proof. Note the difference between proof and persuasion. Some disallow this
distinction, regarding it as a mere play on words. "Are
they not one and the same thing?" they ask. "Is not
something that is proven also necessarily assured?"

Surely it should be so. If a matter is clearly proven,
we ought to be assured of its truthfulness. However,
it does not always work that way. Because of the sin
that clouds our minds and shades our thinking, we are
not always persuaded of truth even in the presence of
incontrovertible and compelling proof. People often
doubt matters which have been conclusively proven.
Jesus himself remarked that some would not believe
even if they saw a person rise from the dead.

Proof is an objective matter subject to the laws
of reason and evidence. Persuasion is a subjective

matter having to do with inner assurance. A syllogism can prove a conclusion is valid, but it cannot yield peace and assurance in a person's heart.

We experience different levels of assurance about different questions. Ask people if they think God exists and you may receive the following replies: "No, definitely not"; "I don't think so"; "I don't know for sure"; "I think so"; "Yes"; or even "Of course." Each reply reveals a different level of assurance or the lack of it.

Calvin goes on to say:

> Nothing, therefore, can be more absurd than the fiction, that the power of judging Scripture is in the Church, and that on her nod its certainty depends. When the Church receives it, and gives it the stamp of her authority, she does not make that authentic which was otherwise doubtful or controverted, but, acknowledging it as the truth of God, she, as in duty bound, shows her reverence by an unhesitating assent. As to the question, How shall we be persuaded that it came from God without referring to a decree of the Church? it is just the same as if were asked, How shall we learn to distinguish light from darkness, white from black, sweet from bitter? Scripture bears upon the face of it

as clear evidence of its truth, as white and black do of their colour, sweet and bitter of their taste.[2]

Calvin was a keen student of church history. He knew that when the Church established the canon of Sacred Scripture she used the Latin word *recipimus*, meaning "we receive. . . ."[3] The Church did not create the canon; the Church received the canon, bowing before the authority integral to it.

When Calvin says that "Scripture bears upon the face of it as clear evidence of its truth . . . ," he is referring to what theologians call the *autopisti* of the Bible. The term *autopisti* means the "self-faith" of the Bible and refers in part to the testimony the Bible gives to its own authority.

The Bible's claim to be the Word of God does not make it the Word of God. Some spurious books make the same claim. *Autopisti* refers not only to the Bible's claim to divine authority but also to the internal marks of its divine character. Calvin notes, for example, the heavenliness of the matter of Scripture, its simplicity, eloquence, miracles, fulfilled prophecy, antiquity, scope, the credibility of its witnesses, etc. Calvin calls these marks the *indicia* of Scripture, things that indicate or point to its divinity.

These marks may "prove" the truthfulness of Scripture, but they do not necessarily persuade men of the truth. Calvin says:

> Our faith in doctrine is not established until we have a perfect conviction that God is its author. Hence, the highest proof of Scripture is uniformly taken from the character of him whose word it is. . . . If, then, we would consult most effectually for our consciences, and save them from being driven about in a whirl of uncertainty, from wavering, and even stumbling at the smallest obstacle, our conviction of the truth of Scripture must be derived from a higher source than human conjectures, judgments, or reasons; namely the secret testimony of the Spirit.[4]

Calvin has been accused of positing confidence in Scripture as an act of blind faith that rests on subjective prejudice, as if he had been heard saying, "The Bible is the Word of God because I believe it to be the Word of God."

Nothing could be further from Calvin's intent or actual teaching. To say that something is true simply because we believe it is not only sheer subjectivism; it is the lowest form of arrogance. It allows the proof of truth to rest in the one claiming it. Calvin is not appealing to the internal testimony of John Calvin; he is appealing to the internal testimony of the Holy Spirit.

For Calvin the testimony of the Holy Spirit is not an inner whisper of new information or an internal trick that changes a poor argument into a good one. The internal testimony does not cause us to believe against evidence; it works in our hearts to cause us to surrender to objective evidence. Calvin uses the word *acquiesce*.[5] We acquiesce *to* the indicia. We do not leap over it or believe against it. In other words, the Spirit causes us to be persuaded *by* the proof.

Calvin acknowledges that a clear objective case for Scripture can be made without appeal to the internal testimony:

> True, were I called to contend with the craftiest despisers of God, I trust, though I am not possessed of the highest ability or eloquence, I should not find it difficult to stop their obstreperous mouths; I could, without much ado, put down the boastings which they mutter in corners, were anything to be gained by refuting their cavils.[6]

Again, Calvin is speaking of the difference between proof and persuasion, between intellectual cogency and the assurance of the heart:

> But although we maintain the sacred Word of God against gainsayers, it does not follow that we shall forthwith implant the certainty which faith requires in their hearts. Profane men think that religion rests only on opinion, and, therefore, that they may not believe foolishly, or on slight grounds desire and insist to have it proved by reason that Moses and the prophets were divinely inspired. But I answer that the testimony of the Spirit is superior to reason. For as God alone can properly bear witness to his own words, so these words will not obtain full credit in the hearts of men, until they are sealed by the inward testimony of the Spirit. The same Spirit, therefore, who spoke by the mouth of the prophets, must penetrate our hearts, in order to convince us that they faithfully delivered the message with which they were divinely intrusted.[7]

When Calvin says that the testimony of the Spirit is superior to reason, he by no means sinks into irrationality. The testimony of the Spirit is *higher* than rationality, not lower. It may be supra-rational, but never irrational. It goes beyond reason, not against it.

When Edwards spoke of the divine and supernatural light, he placed the accent on the excellency that the things of God wrought within the heart. Yet Edwards included the conviction of the truth of Scripture as an integral element of that light. He went beyond Calvin, but not against him. Both agree that it is the inner work of the Holy Spirit that assures us of the divine character of the Word of God.

Calvin also was careful to distinguish the testimony of the Holy Spirit from fresh revelation. He says:

> Those who, rejecting Scripture, imagine that they have some peculiar way of penetrating to God, are to be deemed not so much under the influence of error as madness. For certain giddy men have lately appeared, who, while they make a great display of the superiority of the Spirit, reject all reading of the Scriptures themselves, and deride the simplicity of those who only delight in what they call the dead and deadly letter. But I wish they would tell me what spirit it is whose inspiration raises

them to such a sublime height that they dare despise the doctrine of Scripture as mean and childish.[8]

Apparently the Church will suffer from the influence of "giddy men" in every generation. There seems to be no end to madmen who claim private revelations by which they seduce the lambs and torture the sheep.

Calvin asks:

> But what kind of Spirit did our Saviour promise to send? One who should not speak of himself (John XVI.13), but suggest and instill the truths which he himself had delivered through the word. Hence the office of the Spirit promised to us, is not to form new and unheard-of revelations, or to coin a new form of doctrine, by which we may be led away from the received doctrine of the gospel, but to seal on our minds the very doctrine which the gospel recommends.[9]

Calvin and Edwards both believed that to grow in spiritual light and spiritual life one must seek the Spirit in and through the Word, not apart from it:

Hence it is easy to understand that we must give diligent heed both to the reading and hearing of Scripture, if we would obtain any benefit from the Spirit of God. . . . For the Lord has so knit together the certainty of his word and his Spirit, that our minds are duly imbued with reverence for the word when the Spirit shining upon it enables us there to behold the face of God; and on the other hand, we embrace the Spirit with no danger of delusion when we recognize him in his image, that is, in his word.[10]

THE SCRIPTURAL VIEW OF DIVINE ILLUMINATION:

We have seen how Edwards and Calvin expounded the doctrine of the illumination of the Holy Spirit. Let us turn our attention now to the biblical foundation for the doctrine. The classical treatment is found in Paul's first letter to the Corinthians:

"But as it is written, Eye hath not seen, nor ear heard, neither have entered into the heart of man, the things which God hath prepared for them that love him." (1 Corinthians 2:9)

Just as Jesus told Peter that his recognition of Jesus as the Messiah was not achieved by "flesh and blood" but was revealed to him by God, so Paul stresses the divine origin of the revelation he discloses. He writes:

"That your faith should not stand in the wisdom of men, but in the power of God. Howbeit we speak wisdom among them that are perfect: yet not the wisdom of this world, nor of the princes of this world, that come to nought: but we speak the wisdom of God in a mystery, even the hidden wisdom, which God ordained before the world unto our glory; which none of the princes of this world knew: for had they known it, they would not have crucified the Lord of glory." (1 Corinthians 2:5-8)

Paul contrasts the wisdom that comes from God with wisdom acquired through human means. Worldly wisdom comes to nothing. It lacks ultimate value. From the divine perspective it lacks substance and enduring worth.

Ignorance of spiritual wisdom is both pivotal and catastrophic. Such ignorance precipitated the most heinous crime ever committed. It was out of spiritual ignorance that men crucified the Lord of glory.

We note in the New Testament a temporary divine forbearance with such spiritual ignorance. Jesus prayed for the Father's forgiveness for his killers on the grounds that they did not know what they were doing. Though committed in ignorance, his execution was a monstrous evil.

Peter, in his second sermon in Acts, echoes the ignorance theme:

"And now, brethren, I know that through ignorance ye did it, as did also your rulers." (Acts 3:17)

Likewise, Stephen, in his speech before the Sanhedrin, speaks of the ignorance of the Israelites in the days of Moses:

"For he supposed his brethren would have understood how that God by his hand would deliver them; but they understood not." (Acts 7:25)

Like Jesus before him, Stephen in his hour of death prayed for the forgiveness of his accusers, saying:

"Lord, lay not this sin to their charge." (Acts 7:60)

This ignorance was not based upon a lack of divine revelation. The revelation was there, but it was not spiritually discerned. The ignorance mitigated the guilt of those who killed Jesus and Stephen but did not eliminate it.

Roman Catholic moral theology correctly distinguishes between *vincible ignorance* and *invincible ignorance*. Invincible ignorance is the kind that cannot possibly be overcome. Such ignorance excuses a person from culpability altogether. Vincible ignorance, on the other hand, does not excuse because it is due to neglect and inattention to clear and present revelation. It is an ignorance that *could* have and *should* have been overcome. A person acting in vincible ignorance is morally culpable for his or her actions.

Applying this principle to the crucifixion we say that the people who conspired to slay the Lord of glory did not know whom they were killing, but they *should* have known. His identity had been clearly and marvelously attested by God. Peter declares:

"Ye men of Israel, hear these words; Jesus of Nazareth, a man approved of God among you by miracles and wonders and signs, which God did by him in the midst of you, as ye yourselves also know: Him, being delivered by the determinate counsel and foreknowledge of God, ye have taken, and by wicked hands have crucified and slain." (Acts 2:22-23)

Paul gives the same sort of rebuke to King Agrippa:

"For the king knoweth of these things, before whom also I speak freely: for I am persuaded that none of these things are hidden from him; for this thing was not done in a corner.

"King Agrippa, believest thou the prophets? I know that thou believest. Then Agrippa said unto Paul, Almost thou persuadest me to be a Christian." (Acts 26:26-28)

Spiritual discernment is neither a new revelation nor an understanding that takes place in a vacuum. Prior to spiritual discernment there is an objective divine revelation that is plain for anybody to see. Christianity is not an esoteric religion attainable only by an elite group who alone are privy to divine truth. The revelation of the Lord of Glory takes place in the open sphere of history. It is not a secret thing "done in a corner." No one exposed to the biblical testimony can justly claim ignorance as an excuse for ignorance.

Though God displayed patience toward ignorance for a time, there was a limit, a terminal point, to his forbearance. The Resurrection marked a watershed of divine tolerance to willful human ignorance. Once God fully and finally demonstrated the identity of his Son by raising him from the dead, his forbearance ended:

"And the times of this ignorance God winked at; but now commandeth all men every where to repent: Because he hath appointed a day, in the which he will judge the world in righteousness by that man whom he hath ordained; whereof he hath given assurance unto all men, in that he hath raised him from the dead." (Acts 17:30-31)

Peter and Paul both called people to repent of their ignorance. If ignorance requires repentance, it must be sinful and guilt-bearing. In Old Testament Law, specific trespass offerings were required for sins committed in ignorance.

SPIRITUAL DISCERNMENT

Because it is possible to be exposed to divine revelation and yet remain ignorant of it, something else is required for us to discern it. That "something else" is the illumination of the Holy Spirit:

"But God hath revealed them unto us by his Spirit: for the Spirit searcheth all things, yea, the deep things of God. For what man knoweth the things of a man, save the spirit of man which is in him? even so the things of God knoweth no man, but the Spirit of God." (1 Corinthians 2:10-11)

THE SEARCHING OF THE SPIRIT

What does the apostle mean when he declares that the Spirit searches all things? When we use the word *search* in ordinary language we usually mean actively looking for something that is lost or unknown. However, when the Bible speaks of the Spirit's searching it does not mean that the Holy Spirit is pursuing knowledge that he lacks. The Spirit doesn't search the mind of the Father to discover what is concealed from him there. As the third person of the Trinity, the Holy Spirit partakes of all of the attributes belonging to deity. One such attribute is omniscience. The Holy Spirit knows everything. There is no deficiency in his knowledge. What the Father knows the Spirit knows, as does the Son, the second person of the Trinity. The Spirit then, being omniscient, does not search the things of God as a student searches for new information.

The point of analogy is this: As we use a lamp to search for something in the dark, so the Spirit serves as a lamp for us. As the lamp helps us in our search, so does our spiritual lamp, the Holy Spirit himself. He does not search the mind of God for his benefit; he searches the mind of God for our benefit.

The term *divine illumination* uses a figure of speech drawn from human experience. To "illumine" is to shed light upon. The Spirit is our searchlight who illumines the mind of God for us. He is the one who enlightens the spiritually ignorant.

People can "know us" from the outside by observing us or reading our dossiers. But no one can know us intimately unless we choose to reveal our inner selves. The only one who really knows (apart from God) what is going on inside my mind is myself. So no one knows what's in the mind of God except the Spirit of God. If we are to know and understand the divine mind, we require the assistance of the Holy Spirit:

"Now we have received, not the spirit of the world, but the spirit which is of God; that we might know the things that are freely given to us of God. Which things also we speak, not in the words which man's wisdom teacheth, but which the Holy Ghost teacheth; comparing spiritual things with spiritual. But the natural man receiveth not the things of the Spirit of God: for they are foolishness unto him: neither can he know them, because they are spiritually discerned." (1 Corinthians 2:12-14)

Paul speaks of the believer who has received the Spirit of God. The Spirit of God stands in stark contrast to the spirit of the world. To receive the Spirit means to have him dwelling within us.

There are several redemptive purposes for the indwelling of the Holy Spirit. One is that the indwelling Spirit who regenerates us abides within us to work for our sanctification. Another is that "we might know the things that are freely given to us of God." Here the express purpose is to gain knowledge of God. It is for divine teaching and spiritual discernment that the Holy Spirit takes up residence within us.

Paul concludes his teaching on the subject by writing:

"But he that is spiritual judgeth all things, yet he himself is judged of no man. For who hath known the mind of the Lord, that he may instruct him? But we have the mind of Christ." (1 Corinthians 2:15-16)

Paul's concluding clause is nothing less than astonishing. Its provocative assertion staggers the imagination. "We have the mind of Christ."

Herein lies the greatest possible aid to sanctification—to have at our disposal the very mind of Christ. To have Christ's mind is to think like Christ, to see things from his perspective, to love what Christ loves and to hate what Christ hates, and to be united to his system of values.

Is the goal of Christian living to be Christlike? If so, we will reach that goal only to the degree that we possess the mind of Christ. If, as the Bible declares, as a man thinketh in his heart, so is he, then to the degree that we *think* like Christ, we will *be* like Christ.

Spiritual light is the light of Christ, his teaching, imparted directly to us by his Spirit. Divine illumination is like having Jesus as our personal tutor.

JESUS AS ILLUMINATOR

What happens to people who have the Scriptures opened to them by the Lord of Scripture? The New Testament offers a poignant example.

Luke gives the account of the appearance of the risen Christ to the men on the road to Emmaus. Two disciples departed from Jerusalem after the events surrounding Jesus' death. As they walked toward Emmaus discussing the events, Jesus approached and fell in step with them. However, their eyes were prevented from recognizing him. Jesus questioned them:

"What manner of communications are these that ye have one to another, as ye walk, and are sad? And the one of them, whose name was Cleopas, answering said unto him, Art thou only a stranger in Jerusalem, and hast not known the things which are come to pass there in these days? And he said unto them, What things? And they said unto him, Concerning Jesus of Nazareth, which was a prophet mighty in deed and word before God and all the people." (Luke 24:17-19)

Luke must have chuckled when he related this conversation. Perhaps even Jesus was amused by the circumstances. He played dumb before these men as they instructed him about his own experience.

The men related their account of Jesus' trial and crucifixion and even reported the testimony of the women who had discovered the empty tomb. They added:

"And certain of them which were with us went to the sepulchre, and found it even so as the women had said: but him they saw not." (Luke 24:24)

Jesus responded to their account with a stern rebuke for their foolish ignorance and unbelief:

"O fools, and slow of heart to believe all that the prophets have spoken: Ought not Christ to have suffered these things, and to enter into his glory?" (Luke 24:25-26)

Following this stinging reprimand, Jesus set about to explain the Scriptures to them. Here is spiritual illumination in its most sublime form. Here the Word of God incarnate explains the Word of God written.

"And beginning at Moses and all the prophets, he expounded unto them in all the Scriptures the things concerning himself." (Luke 24:27)

There is no reason to think Jesus added any new content to Scripture. He enlightened them by expounding and illumining the Scripture they already knew.

When they arrived in Emmaus, Jesus joined the men for the evening meal. As he broke bread with them he blessed it. At that moment their eyes were opened in full recognition of his identity. Then he vanished from their sight. The men, obviously excited, recounted to one another what they had just experienced:

"Did not our heart burn within us, while he talked with us by the way, and while he opened to us the Scriptures?" (Luke 24:32)

Here we see it. After the message of God was illumined by the mind of Christ, by the immediate presence of the divine and supernatural light, their hearts were inflamed. John Wesley testified to this in his experience at Aldersgate when, during an exposition from Romans, he sensed that his heart was "strangely warmed."

With their new *understanding* of the Word of

God, the men of Emmaus had a new *love* for it kindled in their hearts. They beheld the excellency of Christ and tasted the sweetness of his words.

It is the Christian who has a burning heart, a soul inflamed, who finds the "something extra" in the Christian life.

5

LOVING
THE LAW
OF GOD

*W*HO LOVES THE LAW OF GOD? IS
God's law merely a burdensome curse
that has at last been sent to the gallows? Is the law
odious to us as the enemy of grace? Is the law an
outmoded way of salvation whose failure is applauded
by the Christian?

Is our devotion to God now conceived in terms of
lawless love, or is there an abiding function of the
Law in the life of the Christian? Does the Old
Testament still instruct us in any way?

Sometimes the Old Testament seems anachronis-
tic. It expresses sentiments that seem ancient to us
and concerns that seem foreign to our thinking.
Consider, for example, these lines from Psalm 119:

"O how love I thy law! It is my meditation all the
day. Thou through thy commandments hast made

me wiser than mine enemies: for they are ever with me. I have more understanding than all my teachers: for thy testimonies are my meditation. I understand more than the ancients, because I keep thy precepts. I have refrained my feet from every evil way, that I might keep thy word. . . . How sweet are thy words unto my taste! yea, sweeter than honey to my mouth." (vv. 97-103)

These strange sounding words express a deep affection for the Law of God. Indeed the whole of Psalm 119, the longest of the psalms, is a panegyric to the Law of God. Where is the Christian who sings such lyrical praises to God's Law? Aren't we more apt to say, "O, how I hate thy Law! How happy am I to be delivered from it!"

Looking closely at the psalm we see a constant interplay between the idea of the Law of God and the Word of God. The two concepts are used interchangeably in the text.

We tend to think of the Law as a specific part, or subdivision, of the broader context of Scriptures. There is nothing wrong with this, as Scripture itself often distinguishes among the Law, the Prophets, and the writings. Therefore, in a narrow sense it is appropriate to distinguish between the Law and other portions of the Word of God. However, in the broad sense the two are to be identified as one. Not only is all of the written Law of God also the written Word of God, it is equally true that all of the Word of God is also the Law of God.

We see parallels to this in our language. It may be said of a ruler or a person in authority that "His word is law." So it is with God. Whatever he says is law to us. His entire Word imposes a sacred obligation upon us that carries with it both duty and responsibility.

If we love the Word of God, we must therefore love the Law of God, both in the broad and in the narrow senses. The psalmist's affection is not directed to the Law of God in abstraction. He loves it because he loves God, and the Law comes from him. He says "I love *thy* Law."

Love for the Law of God is rooted in the relationship between the Law and the lawgiver. God does not learn the Law from some cosmic legal manual and then pass it along to us. Rather the Law of God comes from within him, from his own internal character. It is a reflection of his own righteousness.

PSALM 119

A. F. Kirkpatrick, who wrote at the beginning of the twentieth century, describes this psalm as follows:

This great "Psalm of the Law" is based upon the prophetic (Ezra IX.11) presentation of the Law in the Book of Deuteronomy, with the spirit and language of which its author's mind was saturated. It represents the religious ideas of Deuteronomy developed in the communion of a devout soul with God. . . . The Psalmist is one whose earnest desire and steadfast purpose is to make God's law the governing principle of his conduct, to surrender all self-willed thoughts and aims, to subordinate his whole life to the supremely perfect will of God, with unquestioning faith in his all-embracing providence and unfailing love. . . . It is the "Psalm of the saints; the alphabet of divine love; the Christian's golden ABC of the praise, love, power, and use of the Word of God."[1]

Psalm 119 was written by a Jew during a period of Israelite history marked by a degenerating culture, moral laxity, and secularization. The sentiments expressed in the psalm were greeted, even in the religious community, by hostility and ridicule. The psalmist did not reflect the spirit of his age. He was a spiritual nonconformist, marching to the beat of a different drummer: God.

Nor was the psalmist's devotion a matter of ritual.

The Torah has always been highly esteemed by Jewish people. Every Jewish boy goes through the ceremony called *bar mitzvah*, which means "son of the commandment." At age thirteen the young boy embraces an adult commitment to the Law of God. For many it is merely a traditional ceremony, but for the author of Psalm 119 it was a matter of deepest life. He was, in every true respect, a son of the commandment.

Psalm 119 contains twenty-two complete stanzas, each representing a different letter of the Hebrew alphabet. Each stanza contains eight verses all beginning with the Hebrew letter that stanza represents. The psalm moves through the alphabet consecutively.

Aleph

"Blessed are the undefiled in the way, who walk in the law of the LORD." (v. 1)

The first stanza begins the psalm with a divine benediction. *Blessed* is the word Jesus used at Peter's confession and to introduce the Beatitudes. The psalm begins with the same word the entire book of Psalms begins with—*Blessed*. The blessing is pronounced upon those who walk in the Law of the Lord.

Beth

The second stanza celebrates the joy and delight derived from God's Law:

"I have rejoiced in the way of thy testimonies, as much as in all riches." (v. 14)

This stanza also contains the well-known verse:

"Thy word have I hid in mine heart, that I might not sin against thee." (v. 11)

God's Law, or his Word, is meant to penetrate the secret chambers of the heart, not merely be displayed externally like words chiseled in stone or written on parchment. The sentiment of the psalmist is the goal of the New Testament Christian: to have the Law of God written on our hearts.

Note that in these first two stanzas there is a fresh theme in each one. Rather than give an exposition of all twenty-two stanzas, I will look at a selected portion of the remainder.

"Horror hath taken hold upon me because of the wicked that forsake thy law. Thy statutes have been my songs in the house of my pilgrimage." (vv. 53-54)

Some might get the idea that the psalmist is a legalist or one suffering from a "holier than thou" attitude. He expresses horror at those who have forsaken God's Law, but he is no legalist. To love the Law of God and to keep it is not legalism; it is obedience. The psalmist's horror is not born of a judgmental spirit; it is born of grief over the wholesale neglect of the Law by God's people. Horror should always be the response to antinomianism (anti-lawism).

"It is good for me that I have been afflicted; that I might learn thy statutes." (v. 71)

Affliction is seen by the psalmist not as a calamity, nor as an occasion for bitterness, but as a kind of discipline through which he can learn obedience.

"Thy word is a lamp unto my feet, and a light unto my path." (v. 105)

This famous passage highlights the function of the Law as spiritual light and guidance. We are by nature children of darkness. We are like people without torches called to traverse a treacherous rocky path on a moonless night. We stumble and fall and, far worse, take a detour off the road. It is the psalmist Paul quotes when he says:

"They are all gone out of the way, they are together become unprofitable; there is none that doeth good, no, not one." (Romans 3:12)

This universal indictment of human depravity is that we have gone "out of the way." We have departed from the pathway God commanded us to take. Before Christians were called "Christians" (originally a term of derision), they were called "People of the Way." Hence the image of the path, or roadway, is central to biblical teaching.

The psalmist understood that to keep his feet upon the roadway of God, he must be able to see the road clearly. So he rejoiced that the path was illumined by God's Word. The Word serves as the light that pierces the darkness and allows feet to walk safely.

Jesus himself as the incarnate Word is called the light of the world:

"That was the true Light, which lighteth every man that cometh into the world." (John 1:9)

When Christ appeared to Paul on the road to Damascus and commissioned him to be the apostle to the Gentiles, he said:

"To open their eyes, and to turn them from darkness to light. . . ." (Acts 26:18)

Further testimony to the marvelous character of God's Law is seen in the following texts:

"Thy testimonies are wonderful: therefore doth my soul keep them." (v. 129)

"Thy righteousness is an everlasting righteousness, and thy law is the truth." (v. 142)

In verse 129 the psalmist refers to the "testimonies" of God. This idea is used twenty-three times in Psalm 119. Kirkpatrick notes that the idea of the word is

> that of an attestation, or formal affirmation; hence, as referred to God, a solemn declaration of His will on points (especially) of moral or religious duty, or a protest against human propensity to deviate from it. The word came to be used as a general designation of moral and religious ordinances, conceived as a Divinely instituted standard of conduct.[2]

The term *testimony* is used in the Old Testament as a kind of abbreviation for the Decalogue, or Ten Commandments. The college I attended had the text of Isaiah 8:16 on its official college seal: "Bind up the testimony, seal the law among my disciples."

The psalmist calls the testimonies "wonderful" and the keeping of them a matter of the soul.

The truth of verse 142 was the focal point of one

of my most traumatic moments in seminary. During my first semester the school held an academic convocation, and the speaker was an Old Testament scholar of international reputation. He was one of the original "Quiz Kids" of radio fame. In his address he argued that all of the Old Testament Law was done away with by the New Testament, including the moral law.

His thesis generated immediate controversy, and it spilled over into the next class period, which for me was New Testament Greek. The professor dispatched with parsing and translation work, choosing instead to let the class discuss the issue of the Law.

I stayed out of the discussion until one student asked the professor to have me repeat what I had said to him in the hall on the way to class.

"Well, Mr. Sproul, what do you have to say?" the professor inquired. In halting terms I managed to say, "If the moral law is a reflection of the character of God and the character of God never changes, it seems to me that the moral law wouldn't change either."

At that moment the professor who had given the controversial address walked past our classroom, and the Greek professor called him in. Then, turning to me, the Greek professor said, "Mr. Sproul, tell him what you just said to me."

When I did, the Old Testament professor became

livid and expressed fury at me. He said, "Who do you think you are? You are not an expert in these matters."

I snapped right back at him, "Who do you think you are, to presume to change the eternal character of God." An embarrassed silence enshrouded the room. The Old Testament professor turned and stormed out.

I was wishing for a hole to crawl into when I heard the Greek professor say, in a tender manner, "Mr. Sproul, I'm sorry to have put you on the spot. I think you need to go and speak privately with him."

I was excused from Greek class and began my solitary walk to the Old Testament professor's office. When I apologized to him, his manner turned warm and he, too, apologized. It all worked out fine, but it was an experience I didn't care to repeat.

Just as I still recall the upset of that episode, I still recall the theological issue as well. Though I'm now older and, I hope, wiser, I haven't changed my view, and I find comfort in knowing that the psalmist held the same position. He says that the righteousness of God is an everlasting righteousness. An everlasting righteousness is a righteousness that is neither augmented nor diminished. It does not change. God never goes through an alteration in his holy character.

When the psalmist adds, "and thy law is the

truth," he is basing that judgment on the reality that the Law reflects the everlasting righteousness of God. He confirms this in verse 160:

"Thy word is true from the beginning: and every one of thy righteous judgments endureth for ever."

In spite of such sentiments, numerously expressed in Scripture, a myth persists in our day that the gospel abolishes the Law of God forever. We say "to the gallows with Moses," as if the mediator of the Old Covenant was more oppressive than the Egyptian pharaoh he battled against. The ancient heresy of antinomianism is firmly entrenched in the modern church. The New Covenant is often viewed not in continuity with the Old Covenant but in radical disjunction. The Law is seen as antiquated, passé, and even as a detriment to Christian growth. We are not under the Law, some insist; we are under grace.

That statement, though true in one sense, can be distorted into a perverted creed. The New Covenant, as well as any covenant we have with God, includes stipulations. It was Jesus, not Moses, who said, "If ye love me, keep my commandments" (John 14:15). He added:

"He that hath my commandments, and keepeth them, he it is that loveth me: and he that loveth me shall be loved of my Father, and I will love him, and will manifest myself to him." (John 14:21)

In his Sermon on the Mount, Jesus made a crucial distinction regarding the Law:

"Think not that I am come to destroy the law, or the prophets: I am not come to destroy, but to fulfill. For verily I say unto you, Till heaven and earth pass, one jot or one tittle shall in no wise pass from the law, till all be fulfilled. Whosoever therefore shall break one of these least commandments, and shall teach men so, he shall be called the least in the kingdom of heaven: but whosoever shall do and teach them, the same shall be called great in the kingdom of heaven." (Matthew 5:17-19)

These are weighty words by Jesus. He warns us not to think in antinomian terms. His agenda was not to "loose" or destroy the Law. Nor did he "destroy" the Law by fulfilling it. In this fulfillment, obviously certain aspects of the Law were abrogated. The ceremonies that pointed to Christ's future sacrifice are clearly abrogated, even as are the Old Testament dietary laws. Yet the moral essence of the Law remains as a revelation of what is pleasing to God. He insists that we are not to break even the least of the divine commandments, nor are we to teach others to do so.

By fulfilling the demands of the Law for us, Christ removed the curse of the Law from us. We are delivered from the miserable burden of the Law, its punitive sanctions. This does not mean, however, that we are given a license for lawlessness. Lawlessness is the trademark of the antichrist.

The apostle Paul in both Romans and Galatians belabors the point that the Law cannot justify us; it can only condemn us. We are justified by faith and not through the works of the Law. We who are redeemed from the curse of the Law are not to "marry it" (i.e., look to the Law as a way of salvation). The Law exposes our sin and points us to our need of a Savior.

Yet Paul also emphasizes that there is nothing faulty about the Law. Yes, it is impotent to save us, but that was never its purpose. It is not impotent to teach us righteousness and to reveal what is pleasing to God. The fault is not with the Law; the fault lies with us. Paul writes:

"Wherefore the law is holy, and the commandment holy, and just, and good. . . . For we know that the law is spiritual." (Romans 7:12, 14)

It is the spiritual import of the Law that is vitally

important for the Christian. One cannot become spiritual by the Law, but we can learn the way of spiritual obedience from the Law.

One of the most important contributions John Calvin made to the Protestant Reformation was his explanation of the role the Law plays in the life of a Christian. Calvin delineated a threefold function, or use, of the Law.

THE FIRST FUNCTION OF THE LAW

> First, by exhibiting the righteousness of God—in other words, the righteousness which alone is acceptable to God—it admonishes every one of his own unrighteousness, certiorates, convicts, and finally condemns him. This is necessary, in order that man, who is blind and intoxicated with self-love, may be brought at once to know and to confess his weakness and impurity.[3]

Calvin echoes Paul's teaching that the Law is a schoolmaster to bring us to Christ (Galatians 3:24). The *pedagogue* is the strict disciplinarian who raps our knuckles with a ruler when we misbehave. Calvin adds:

If we look merely to the Law, the result must
be despondency, confusion, and despair, seeing
that by it we are all cursed and condemned,
while we are kept far away from the blessedness
which it holds forth to its observers.[4]

Calvin likens the first function of the Law to a
mirror:

As in a mirror we discover any stains upon our
face, so in the Law we behold, first, our impotence; then, in consequence of it, our iniquity;
and finally, the curse, as the consequence of
both.[5]

Calvin then quotes passages from Saint Augustine
which utter this theme:

The utility of the law is, that it convinces man
of his weakness, and compels him to apply for
the medicine of grace, which is in Christ.[6]

Again, quoting Augustine:

God enjoins what we cannot do, in order that
we may know what we have to ask of him. . . .
The law was given, that it might make you

guilty—being made guilty, might fear; fearing, might ask indulgence, not presume on your own strength.[7]

Finally, from Augustine:

> The law was given, in order to convert a great into a little man.[8]

The Law converts great men into little men! This is the essence of the first function of the Law.

THE SECOND FUNCTION OF THE LAW

Calvin's second function of the Law is to act as a restraint against unbridled wickedness. Just as speed limit signs put legal restraints upon reckless drivers, so the Law of God, with its threat of punishment, curbs us from wanton moral abandonment. Calvin writes:

> The second office of the Law is, by means of its fearful denunciations and the consequent dread of punishment, to curb those who, unless forced, have no regard for rectitude and justice. Such persons are curbed, not because their mind is inwardly moved and affected, but

because, as if a bridle were laid upon them, they refrain their hands from external acts, and internally check the depravity which would otherwise petulantly burst forth.[9]

The restraining function of the Law does not mellow the heart of the one restrained. On the contrary, the more one is restrained by Law, the more hostile to the Law the person becomes. Here is irony and paradox. On the one hand, the Law does restrain; on the other hand, it incites and inflames toward sin. Paul writes:

"But sin, taking occasion by the commandment, wrought in me all manner of concupiscence. For without the law sin was dead." (Romans 7:8)

Calvin comments:

Nay, the more they restrain themselves, the more they are inflamed, the more they rage and boil, prepared for any act or outbreak whatsoever, were it not for the furor of the law. And not only so, but they thoroughly detest the law itself, and execrate the Lawgiver; so that if they could, they would most willingly annihilate him, because they cannot bear either his ordering what is right, or his avenging the despises of his Majesty.[10]

THE THIRD FUNCTION
OF THE LAW

According to Calvin, the *tertius usus*, or "third use," of the Law was most important for the Christian in whom the Holy Spirit dwells. This we call the *revelatory function* of the Law. Here the Law functions in the life of the Christian as it did in the life of the psalmist. Calvin says:

> For it is the best instrument for enabling them daily to learn with greater truth and certainty what that will of the Lord is which they aspire to follow, and to confirm them in this knowledge; just as a servant who desires with all his soul to approve himself to his master.[11]

One of the questions most frequently asked of pastors and theologians is the plaintive query, "How can I know the will of God for my life?" It seems as though everyone wants to know the will of God, yet nobody wants to know his Law. This is theological madness. The easiest and best way to learn the will of God is by studying his Law. The Law reveals what pleases God: obedience. God's will for our lives is that we be sanctified.

The Law not only reveals what pleases God, it

propels us along the pathway of obedience. Calvin writes:

> The Law acts like a whip to the flesh, urging it on as men do a lazy sluggish ass. Even in the case of a spiritual man, inasmuch as he is still burdened with the weight of the flesh, the Law is a constant stimulus, pricking him forward when he would indulge in sloth.[12]

The incitement of the Law to obedience is a means of grace for the believer. The Law, once we are regenerate, far from slaying us, now excites our souls to please our Savior. Moses himself understood this when he exhorted the children of Israel:

"Set your hearts unto all the words which I testify among you this day, which ye shall command your children to observe to do, all the words of this law. For it is not a vain thing for you; because it is your life. . . ." (Deuteronomy 32:46-47)

It is the Christian's life! This is the sentiment of any believer who delights in obedience and seeks the blessedness that flows from pleasing God. The believer rejects legalism, while embracing the Law as it still applies. The Law is a clear guide to the way of obedient living. To love God is to obey God.

6

THE
OBEDIENT
SOUL

I N ANY DISCIPLINE WE PURSUE, MODELS
who provide a standard of excellence that we can
pattern ourselves after help us achieve our full potential.
When our models are real people and not mythical
heroes, we have the added benefit of human inspira-
tion. When we see other mortals reaching a high level
in our discipline, we are encouraged to do the same.

The Bible sets forth for our imitation models of
obedience drawn from flesh-and-blood humanity.
For example, the apostle Paul was conscious of his
place as a role model when he wrote: "Be imitators
of me, as I am of Christ" (1 Corinthians 11:1 RSV).

THE MODEL OF MARY

Because of the central, and often cultic, role Mary
plays in Roman Catholic theology, Protestants often

neglect her in their thinking. Yet Mary was chosen to be the mother of Christ. Protestant theology generally agrees with the teaching found in the great ecumenical councils of early church history. This includes embracing the title given to Mary: *Theotokos*, which means "mother of God." In the final analysis, Mary's title was given not so much to honor her as to honor the Son she bore. That Mary was the mother of God simply means that her child was God Incarnate. It does not mean that Mary was the genetrix of Jesus' deity. The "Father" of Jesus in his birth was the Holy Spirit. Yet it was maintained by the early councils that Jesus received his human nature from his mother. He was born of the seed of David, from which Mary came. Yet this human child was also *vere deus*, truly God. His mother was not God, but he was. Therefore, since Jesus was God and Mary was his mother, it is clear that she was indeed the mother of God.

The biblical portrait of Mary is as instructive as it is inspirational. If ever a woman walked this earth whose soul was inflamed with holy things, it was Mary.

MARY'S FIAT

One of the most noteworthy and controversial aspects of Mary's life is found in the episode that contains what Rome calls her *fiat*.

When the angel Gabriel appeared to Mary in Nazareth and announced the impending birth, Mary was shocked and bewildered. She raised the obvious question: "How shall this be, seeing I know not a man?" (Luke 1:34).

When Gabriel patiently explained to Mary that the seemingly impossible would be accomplished by a supernatural work of the Holy Spirit, Mary gave this historic response:

"Behold the handmaid of the Lord; be it unto me according to thy word." (Luke 1:38)

This reply, which rests on the words "Be it unto me," is called "Mary's Fiat." Students of Latin who use the term *fiat* are not referring to a small Italian car. To them a fiat is the imperative form of the Latin verb *to be*. A fiat is a command. When God created the universe by issuing a command, it is said (by Augustine) that he created the world via "divine imperative." Therefore, it is called *fiat creation*.

That Mary altered such a command, or fiat, in her response to Gabriel is an important issue in modern Roman Catholic theology. At Vatican Council II, two factions in the Roman Church engaged in a debate which was not resolved. The two factions (which generally represent the divided thinking between the Latin wing of the church and the Western wing) have been identified as the *Maximalist* wing and the *Minimalist* wing, so called because of the degree of importance they attribute to the role of Mary in the drama of redemption.

The Maximalists push for the title of co-redemptrix for Mary. They insist that Mary had such a positive and necessary role in our redemption that she is worthy to be venerated along with her Son as a co-redeemer. This view (which has not been officially adopted by Rome) stresses what is called the Eve-Mary Parallel.[1]

Just as the New Testament draws a parallel relationship between Adam and Jesus as the Second Adam, so a parallel is drawn between Eve and Mary, the Second Eve. The parallels focus on the question of obedience. As by one man's disobedience the world was plunged into ruin, so by another man's obedience redemption is accomplished. In like manner by one woman's disobedience (Eve's) the fall of mankind occurred, so by another woman's obedience (Mary's) redemption is brought to pass.

The assumption behind this is that the redemption of the world depended upon Mary's decision to accept Gabriel's proposal. Mary exercised her authority in a positive manner by commanding that it "be so." Hence the entire matter of Jesus' entrance into the world rested upon Mary's fiat.

The Minimalist wing takes a different view, one much closer to the classical Protestant view. Mary's fiat is not a command to Gabriel; it is a command to Mary, a command to herself. When she said, "Be it unto me," she was not so much exercising authority as she was submitting to the authority vested in Gabriel as the representative of God.

From our vantage point we see it as crucial that Mary's initial response to Gabriel is in the words "Behold the handmaid of the Lord."

Mary's initial response to Gabriel's declaration was one of clear subservience. She did not describe herself as a "partner" or "peer" of the Lord. She was the Lord's handmaiden, willing and eager to be his servant. Nor did Gabriel offer Mary a proposal, to which Mary was given a moral option to accept or reject. He said:

"The Holy Ghost shall come upon thee, and the power of the Highest shall overshadow thee: therefore also that holy thing which shall be born of thee shall be called the Son of God." (Luke 1:35)

It is to this sovereign announcement that Mary willingly and joyfully acquiesced. Her words comprise a model of godly obedience: "Be it unto me according to thy word." At the risk of belaboring the obvious, it is important to notice that Mary did not say, "Be it unto me according to *my* word." The difference between "thy" and "my" is the difference between obedience and arrogance.

What makes Mary's response a model for us is this: She was willing to have happen to her, and in her, whatever was pleasing to God. She was prepared to submit to the Word of God no matter the risk or cost to herself.

The Christian life is one of willing obedience. The singular command that drives the holy life is the command to submit to whatever God calls us to do.

That Mary was called upon by God to perform a difficult and sacrificial task does not mean that she was an object of divine displeasure or under his curse. Far from it. The initial greeting of Gabriel to Mary captures the estate in which Mary found herself:

"Hail, thou that art highly favoured, the Lord is with thee: blessed art thou among women." (Luke 1:28)

This is the original Ave Maria. The angel's greeting included an announcement of divine benevolence. Mary was "highly favoured." It also included the supreme benediction: *"Blessed* art thou among women."

That Mary was singularly blessed is a theme continued in the birth narratives. For example, of Mary's visit to her cousin Elisabeth, Luke wrote:

"And it came to pass, that, when Elisabeth heard the salutation of Mary, the babe leaped in her womb; and Elisabeth was filled with the Holy Ghost: And she spake out with a loud voice, and said, Blessed art thou among women, and blessed is the fruit of thy womb." (Luke 1:41-42)

The words of Elisabeth, "Blessed art thou among women, and blessed is the fruit of thy womb," are incorporated in the Roman Catholic ritual known as the Rosary, which includes the words:

Hail Mary, full of grace, the Lord is with thee. Blessed art thou among women, and blessed is the fruit of thy womb, Jesus.

Holy Mary, mother of God, pray for us sinners, now and in the hour of our death. Amen.

The Rosary combines words from Elisabeth, Gabriel, and church tradition. We see the accent that stresses the blessedness of Mary.

What of Mary herself? In her own song of praise, the Magnificat, Mary declares,

"For, behold, from henceforth all generations shall call me blessed." (Luke 1:48b)

These words may be regarded as prophetic because, indeed, every generation since the first century has attested to the blessedness of Mary.

The Magnificat, so named because it is the first word in Latin of Mary's song, provides insight into Mary's spiritual character. Mary begins her song with these words:

"My soul doth magnify the Lord, and my spirit hath rejoiced in God my Savior." (Luke 1:46-47)

These opening lines of the Magnificat have profound theological significance concerning Mary's role in redemption. They tend to undermine the Roman dogma of the sinlessness of Mary. Even Saint Thomas Aquinas commented that here Mary acknowledged that God was her Savior. Jesus was not only Mary's son; he was her Savior as well.

It can be, and indeed has been, argued by subsequent Roman theologians that God can be Savior in ways other than being the deliverer from sin. To experience any benefit from the hand of God may be regarded as a kind of salvation without implying redemption from the consequences of sin. They say, therefore, that it is not necessary to infer from this passage that Mary meant God saved her from sin.

The meaning of God's saving act may be discovered in the next verse:

"For he hath regarded the low estate of his handmaiden: for, behold, from henceforth all generations shall call me blessed." (Luke 1:48)

Mary's "salvation" could simply refer to God's rescue of her from her low estate. She is rescued from insignificance and is given unique status and dignity by being selected as the mother of Christ. She moves from total obscurity to become the focus of blessedness throughout church history. In the biblical sense this is no small salvation.

Apart from other theological considerations (especially that there is no governing theological necessity for Mary to have been sinless in order to bear Christ), the context of Mary's words suggests a high probability that her reference to God as her Savior should be taken in the narrow sense as Savior from her sins.

If we push the notion that Mary *had* to be sinless to bear a sinless child (a child free of original sin), then the same logic demands that Anna, the mother of Mary, must likewise have been sinless. This factor plays a role in the Roman doctrine of the Immaculate Conception of Mary. The Immaculate Conception does not refer to the conception of Jesus in the womb of Mary. It refers to the conception of Mary in the womb of her mother, Saint Anne. Again, pushed to its logical conclusion this thesis would require that Anne's conception in the womb of her mother would also have to have been Immaculate, and so on all the way back to Eve. (The issue also touches the theological debate of creationism versus traducianism, which focuses on the means or manner by which original sin is transmitted from parent to child.)

A second factor concerns the use of the term *Savior* in the broader context of the infancy narrative. In the Magnificat, Mary is certainly responding in large part to the Annunciation by Gabriel. Gabriel announces to Mary that her child shall be called "Jesus." When Gabriel reveals this news to Joseph, he gives the reason for the name: "For he shall save his people from their sins" (Matthew 1:21b).

The full content of the Magnificat calls attention to the relationship of the birth of Jesus to the ancient covenant promises God made to Abraham:

"He hath holpen his servant Israel, in remembrance of his mercy; As he spake to our fathers, to Abraham, and to his seed for ever." (Luke 1:54-55)

These words set the theme of the Magnificat squarely in the broader Old Testament context of the history of redemption in the fullest soteriological sense, far beyond mere rescue from social obscurity.

We see then that the Magnificat is a hymn of adoration and praise, as well as a hymn of thanksgiving. In it Mary reveals her own character of spiritual devotion and obedience. The adoration she expresses is not perfunctory; it flows from the depth of her soul. Her Spirit-inspired song makes use of a Hebrew literacy form, parallelism, as she sings:

"My soul doth magnify the Lord, And my spirit hath rejoiced in God my Savior." (Luke 1:46-47)

This is an example of synonymous parallelism whereby the second verse repeats the same thought as the first verse, though employing different words. The two major parallels are "soul" and "spirit," and "magnify" and "rejoice." The joy and magnification Mary expresses in heartfelt passion is characteristic of the model believer.

We could see Mary's response as mere emotionalism that lacks substance. Some people can generate enthusiasm with little understanding. If we examine the record closely, however, it becomes apparent that

Mary's response is not mindless zeal. When her baby was born in Bethlehem, and she and Joseph and the babe were visited by the awestruck shepherds, "Mary kept all these things, and pondered them in her heart" (Luke 2:19).

Spiritual "enthusiasm" is often short-lived. The zeal of some believers is only as strong as the memory of their most recent blessing. By contrast, Mary *kept* these things. She held on to them. They became a matter of deep and abiding reflection.

In compiling data to write his gospel narrative, Luke probably interviewed Mary many years after the events occurred. Luke's insertion of the note that Mary kept and pondered these things is perhaps due to his firsthand report from her.

Luke adds to the infancy narrative an account of Jesus being brought to the temple for dedication and the meeting with Simeon and the prophetess Anna (Luke 2:25-39). In this episode Simeon delivered a prophecy that contained an ominous note:

"And Simeon blessed them, and said unto Mary his mother, Behold, this child is set for the fall and rising again of many in Israel; and for a sign which shall be spoken against; (Yea, a sword shall pierce through thy own soul also;) that the thoughts of many hearts may be revealed." (Luke 2:34-35)

No doubt Mary pondered these words as well. She lived to see the prophecy fulfilled. Mary was an eyewitness to her own son's crucifixion. We can safely assume that when the Roman soldier thrust a spear into Jesus' side that it pierced not only the body of Jesus but the soul of his mother as well.

Mary's "participation" in the agony of her Son did not qualify her as a co-redemptrix. Under similar circumstances any mother would feel her son's pain.

Mary is seen in a multitude of situations that believers encounter. She is a worthy model of devotion, as seen in her humility, obedience, spirit of worship, pensive reflection on the deep things of God, perseverance in faith, and in personal affliction. These are the marks of the Christian.

SHADRACH, MESHACH, AND ABED-NEGO

The Old Testament account by the prophet Daniel of the crises of Shadrach, Meshach, and Abed-nego is another illustration of spiritual devotion. Mary's "fiat" was actually a submission to God's fiat. Here, in contrast, we see the fiat of a godless king, and obeying it required treason against God. The faithful Jews demonstrate the nature of godly obedience even when it entails great cost.

When Nebuchadnezzar, King of Babylon, erected a huge golden image in the plain of Dura, he enacted a decree that everyone was to fall down and worship the image at a given signal. The penalty for failure to comply was to be cast alive into a fiery furnace.

For the devout Jew, compliance with the royal mandate was an act of crass idolatry, and the prohibition against idolatry was absolutely central to Jewish faith.

Compromise is formidably tempting when the alternative is a visit to the furnace, and multitudes of professed Jews obeyed the king instead of God. I am sure they filled themselves with every conceivable rationalization. Some undoubtedly praised themselves for practicing civil obedience.

The response of Shadrach, Meshach, and Abednego, however, was heroic. They boldly confessed their faith to the king, saying:

"O Nebuchadnezzar, we are not careful to answer thee in this matter. If it be so, our God whom we serve is able to deliver us from the burning fiery furnace, and he will deliver us out of thine hand, O king." (Daniel 3:16-17)

With these words the faithful men testified of their confidence in God's ability to redeem them. However, as certain as they were that God was indeed *able* to rescue them, they were not certain that God would in fact do so. They knew history. There were times when God in his providence allowed his people to be martyred, to suffer for righteousness' sake. They were fully prepared for that eventuality. They added a crucial qualifier to their testimony:

"But if not, be it known unto thee, O king, that we will not serve thy gods, nor worship the golden image which thou hast set up." (Daniel 3:18)

The men acknowledged that God had an option. He could choose to intervene on their behalf or not. God was not morally obligated to save them. They understood that. Yet at the same time they recognized that they had no option. They could not compromise. They would not engage in idolatry no matter the cost. Their stand was not the result of a narrow-minded stubbornness or rigidity; integrity was at stake. Nor was it the result of selfish pride; their loyalty to God was the issue. So they chose the furnace over disobedience.

Nebuchadnezzar was not impressed with their devotion. He was so enraged that he ordered the furnace to be heated seven times hotter than usual. This is an ironic testimony to the foolishness of the king. It's like a commander ordering that seven times more sharpshooters be used in a firing squad. The furnace was already hot enough to do the job. It wouldn't matter to Shadrach, Meshach, and Abed-nego how much hotter the furnace became. Indeed it would be a reverse kind of mercy in that the hotter the fire, the quicker their suffering would end. The additional stoking of the furnace was merely an act to satisfy the king's personal fury.

When Shadrach, Meshach, and Abed-nego were hurled into the furnace, the guards who threw them in were immediately consumed. Nebuchadnezzar himself approached the furnace to inspect the results and was astonished by what he observed. He inquired of his counsellors:

"Did not we cast three men bound into the midst of the fire? They answered and said unto the king, True, O king. He answered and said, Lo, I see four men loose, walking in the midst of the fire, and they have no hurt; and the form of the fourth is like the Son of God." (Daniel 3:24-25)

The appearance of the fourth figure in the furnace is mysterious. Nebuchadnezzar's description does not necessarily mean that he recognized the presence of the second person of the Trinity. He may have been referring to an angel. In fact, later he used the word *angel.* Such miraculous intervention would suit the role of an angel (angels are sometimes referred to as "sons of God"), whose tasks include ministering to saints in times of crisis. On the other hand, this text could indicate a cryptic reference to a Christophany, an Old Testament manifestation of the pre-incarnate Christ.

In either case, the fourth figure represents one who is sent by God as a sign of God's own presence in the crisis. Shadrach, Meshach, and Abed-nego were not only comforted in their ordeal by the divine presence; they were rescued altogether from the flames:

"And the princes, governors, and captains, and the king's counsellors, being gathered together, saw these men, upon whose bodies the fire had no power, nor was a hair of their head singed, neither were their coats changed, nor the smell of fire had passed on them." (Daniel 3:27)

The men emerged from the furnace unscathed, without any evidence that they had been near a fire.

The model character of these men is not simply a testimony to God's ability and willingness to rescue his people. More importantly, it is a witness to the saints' confidence in divine providence, no matter what it decrees. Their confession before the king anticipated Mary's fiat: "Be it so unto me according to thy word."

Had the story ended differently, with the bodies of Shadrach, Meshach, and Abed-nego being burned to a crisp, the model of their devotion would still have remained intact. It is a model of obedience of men in a different time and different place from ours, yet their fidelity remains a constant model for us.

7

THE
MODEL
OF JOSEPH

*I*N THE EARLY CHURCH THE APOLOGIST
Justin Martyr appealed to the exemplary lives
of Christians as evidence of the transforming power
of Christ. He gave special prominence to the model
of sexual purity exhibited by Christians. The early
church was not yet seduced by an eroticized culture.
The clear commands of God had been seared on
their consciences.

The call to sexual purity is rooted early in biblical
history. Even before Moses received the Ten Commandments at Sinai, sexual purity was viewed as a
priority of godly conduct. The influence of pagan
nations was not to be permitted to sanction sexual
immorality. The drama of the conflict between
godly behavior and pagan sexual behavior is seen in
the life of the patriarch Joseph. Joseph was put to the
test in a strange and pagan land.

Joseph's pilgrimage from being slave to becoming prime minister of Egypt included spending time in prison. Though innocent, he was incarcerated after his master's wife accused him of attempting to rape her. Genesis describes Joseph as a "goodly person, and well-favoured" (Genesis 39:6). He was especially "well-favoured" by Potiphar's wife, who tried to seduce him:

"And it came to pass after these things, that his master's wife cast her eyes upon Joseph; and she said, Lie with me." (Genesis 39:7)

The woman's invitation to sexual liaison was direct and provocative, and she made this advance not once, but many times.

David, king of Israel, would succumb to temptation in the future, but Joseph did not. And he was careful to explain the reason:

"Behold, my master knoweth not what is with me in the house, and he hath committed all that he hath to my hand; There is none greater in this house than I; neither hath he kept back any thing from me but thee, because thou art his wife: how then can I do this great wickedness, and sin against God?" (Genesis 39:8-9)

Although Joseph was a slave in the house of Potiphar, he evidently had been elevated to a position of authority. Potiphar had invested a high level of trust in his servant, as Joseph had access to all of his master's possessions, with one exception—his wife.

Joseph's conscience was sensitized in two directions. On one hand, he had an obligation to his earthly master. To give in to the request of Potiphar's wife would be to sin against Potiphar and dishonor him.

But there was a more weighty consideration. To become sexually involved with Potiphar's wife would be to commit an offense against the Law of God. When Joseph asked, "How then can I do this great wickedness, and sin against God?" he did not expect a rationalized response from the woman. It was clearly a rhetorical question, and the answer was patently obvious: he could not. There was no possible justification for complying with the request.

Joseph did not deceive himself with convoluted rationalization. His understanding of the Law of God had progressed from consciousness to conviction to conscience.

THE SENSITIZED CONSCIENCE

The conscience has been described by Saint Thomas Aquinas as the inner voice of God by which we are either accused or excused for our actions. It is a kind of internal governor that restrains or allows behavior.

The inner voice of conscience can be muted by repeated sins. We develop internal earmuffs to silence its accusing cries. However, as the Spirit sounds his trumpet in our souls in the process of sanctification, that which has been muffled is now amplified, and we gain ears to hear.

The one who loves the Law of God as the psalmist did is one whose conscience has been awakened to the voice of God and captured by it.

Again, there are stages in the development of a sensitized conscience. It begins with *consciousness*. To love the Law we must first be conscious of it, and our minds must be cognizant of the Law's content. We cannot be convinced of any truth unless we are first aware of that truth. Yet to be aware of the Law is not necessarily to be convinced of its truthfulness or validity. Every day we violate laws that we are aware of. We see the sign along the highway that says Speed Limit 55 mph. At the same time we see the speedometer on our dashboard that indicates 60 mph and know we are breaking the law.

To become obedient to the law we must not only be aware of it, we must become convinced of its truthfulness and validity. (However, we are required to obey the Law of God and the laws of man even if we think they are invalid.) We may think the speed limit is silly, but we are still required, even by God, to obey it. We are required to obey all laws unless they command us to do something God forbids or forbid us from doing something God commands.

To be truly obedient we must become convinced of and acknowledge the principle that requires us to obey laws that we are not sure are valid. To do so requires that we have already gone through the process with respect to another law.

For example, I can be motivated to obey a man-made law even if I am not convinced of its validity because I am aware that God commands me to obey such laws. Because the Law of God is valid and I have become convinced of it, I am constrained to obey human laws even though I am unconvinced of their specific validity.

In other words, if I am aware of a speed limit that I think is foolish, I must obey it out of conscience because I am aware that God commands me to obey the civil magistrates. With respect to God's Law that commands me to obey other laws, I am not only aware that God has so commanded, but I am convinced and captured in conscience that God's Law is valid. Therefore, we can obey specific laws about whose wisdom we are not convinced because of our prior conviction of the superior Law of God.

However, at some point we must go through the stages. We must move from consciousness to conviction if we are to be persuaded and motivated to obey the Law of God.

But this is not enough to restrain us from sin. We may be both aware of a Law of God and fully convinced that it is valid, yet still disobey it. We may agree that the 55 mph speed limit is valid and just. The problem we have is that it conflicts with our personal desires. We want to drive faster. We may be somewhat restrained by fear of getting caught. Or to satisfy our desire yet avoid getting caught, we might take such elaborate measures as installing radar-detecting devices in our cars. This reveals our crass determination and premeditation to be disobedient. And when we complain that it is unfair for the police to use speed traps to catch us in our transgressions, we vividly display our lack of conscience. We argue that the police are "cheating" in their efforts to catch us. Much of the protest against speed traps is based upon a prior protest against the speed limit itself.

Nevertheless, consciousness of a law coupled with conviction of its validity still is not always enough to motivate obedience. A strong motivation to obedience requires another factor: the sensitive conscience.

Joseph was aware of God's law against adultery.

He was convinced of its validity. *And* God's law against adultery had penetrated his conscience.

Joseph's conscience had been awakened to a sense not only of the truth of God's Law but also of its excellency, a process described earlier in our discussion of Jonathan Edwards's doctrine of illumination. An affection for obedience had been quickened within him that touched his will as well as his brain.

A man can be aware of the Law against adultery and even be convinced that the Law is right and good. Yet he still has a conflict. His inner desire to sin is greater than his inner desire to obey God. When that happens, he sins. We can safely and accurately universalize this phenomenon. At the moment we choose to sin, our desire to commit the sin is stronger than our desire to obey God. That, plain and simple, is why we sin. We may have a conflict of desires within ourselves. We may have a general desire to obey Christ. But we have another desire as well: the desire to sin. When our desire to sin exceeds our desire to obey, we sin. When we desire to obey more than we desire to sin, we obey.

Sanctification is a twofold development. On the one hand, the old self with its inclinations to sin is being put to death. On the other hand, the new self with its inclinations to obey is being awakened and strengthened. Only when the spiritual inclinations of the new self are fully developed do we see progress in development.

The bad news is that even when our consciousness of God's Law goes from conviction to conscience, there is still no guarantee that we will obey. David was aware of the law against adultery, and surely he was also convinced of its validity. And the depth of his subsequent repentance shows that he was not without a conscience on the matter. But he managed to numb his conscience until Nathan pricked it. Then he felt its full force.

Conscience vacillates in power from day to day, but it can be strengthened or weakened. Again, the process begins with the mind. The more I increase my awareness of the Law, the more I am convicted of a matter. The greater my conviction, the stronger my conscience. The stronger my conscience, the greater the likelihood that I will obey.

It is not enough to know that God forbids adultery. Nor is it enough to be convinced that God forbids it. We may still fail to grasp how utterly offensive it is to God. We tend to make it a small deal where God sees it as a big deal.

I believe that adultery is wrong. Yet I am encircled by a culture that views it as a relatively small matter.

Societal permissiveness does not jibe with the strong position God takes on the matter. I may be seduced into thinking that, yes, I know it's wrong, but everybody is doing it so it can't be all that bad.

We need to have the mind of Christ on the matter. We would have a lot fewer cases of this particular evil if we had the mind of Joseph on the subject. For him it was an act of treason against God. For Jesus it was altogether unthinkable. This is Calvin's second use of the Law with a vengeance. The mind informed by God's holy Law is restrained from evil. Joseph was so in tune with the priorities of God's Law that he refused to even entertain the thought of adultery. It simply wasn't an option for him. We see a similar scale of priorities in the apostle Paul's command regarding fornication:

"But fornication, and all uncleanness, or covetousness, let it not be once named among you, as becometh saints." (Ephesians 5:3)

Paul says fornication is a sin that shouldn't *ever* occur among Christians. Don't let it *once* be named among you, he implores. How, I wonder, would Paul respond to the sexual climate of America? Surveys indicate that fornication is the national pastime and is epidemic in the church. Certainly it is named more than once among us. Most Christians still regard fornication as a sin, but its seriousness has slid to an all-time low. Fornication and adultery are transgressions on which our consciences have been inadequately sensitized. We have relegated them to the level of a minor sin, a virtual peccadillo.

As a boy I was unregenerate and therefore unchristian. My soul was not disposed to obeying the Law of God. My problem was dealing with the laws of my parents. Some of their laws I obeyed; others I disobeyed. The ones I tended to obey were the ones delivered to me in emphatic terms. For example, one day the woman next door said something to me that I didn't like, and I let her know it. I said, "You're not my mother, so I don't have to listen to you." Unfortunately, my mother heard me utter these words. She said, "Well *I* am your mother and I won't tolerate sassing your elders." She demanded that I apologize to the woman immediately. The message I got was clear: Talking back to my elders was a definite no-no. There was no tolerance for it. I amended my behavior in a hurry once I learned that sassiness was a big deal.

Joseph had been so instructed in the Law of God that he understood adultery was not a negotiable option. God's commandment was so entrenched in his soul that Joseph needed no law enforcement agent to restrain him.

INTERNAL REINFORCEMENT OF THE LAW

Just because a law is enacted does not mean that people will necessarily obey it. And so we must have law enforcement agencies. An enforcement agency is so called because it is authorized to use force to coerce people into obedience. It is not a punitive agency. Punishment is left to the courts.

If we are to be moved to obedience without external agencies of enforcement, we must have the law reinforced within ourselves. Such reinforcement comes to us in essentially three ways.

First, it comes via the Scriptures. By *repeated* study of the Scripture, its message is reinforced to us.

When the psalmist declared that he meditated on the Law day and night, he was describing a process by which he was frequently and repeatedly exposed to the Word of God. His meditation was neither superficial nor occasional. He immersed himself in the Law of God and came to love it. The affections of the Law became the affections of his own heart.

The second means of reinforcement is the divine illumination of the Holy Spirit. When the Spirit convicts of sin and of righteousness, he writes the Law of God upon our hearts.

The command to write the Law upon our hearts

does not refer simply to a new location. Whether the Law is written on tablets of stone or printed on frontlets hanging from our forehead, it is still external to us. When it is written on our hearts, it is internal. Though not as easy to see, it is easier to obey.

The purpose of writing the Law on our hearts is not to enhance its *visibility* but its *viability*. We conclude, then, that to have the Law written on our hearts refers to God's changing the disposition of the heart toward the love of obedience.

Again, God does not write his Law upon our hearts until our minds are first made aware of it. The expression "written on the heart" is used in two different ways in the Bible. The first is with respect to knowledge only. Even the pagan has the Law of God in this respect. Paul writes:

"For when the Gentiles, which have not the law, do by nature the things contained in the law, these, having not the law, are a law unto themselves: Which show the work of the law written in their hearts, their conscience also bearing witness, and their thoughts the mean while accusing or else excusing one another." (Romans 2:14-15)

The apostle is not declaring that pagans have the sanctifying influence of the Spirit. Rather, he is simply asserting that they are not completely ignorant of God's Law. God reveals his Law not only through the light of special revelation, such as that delivered by Moses, but also through nature. This natural revelation is immediate and innate. Though ignorant of the Bible, people have a sense of right and wrong and are endowed with conscience.

The above type of revelation may be referred to as the writing of the Law in the broader and cognitive sense. The narrow and affective sense refers to the sanctifying influence of the Holy Spirit in the heart of the believer.

This narrow and affective sense is what the author of Hebrews has in mind when he alludes to Jeremiah's prophecy of the new covenant:

"For this is the covenant that I will make with the house of Israel after those days, saith the Lord; I will put my laws into their mind, and write them in their hearts: and I will be to them a God, and they shall be to me a people." (Hebrews 8:10)

Here the author of Hebrews echoes the sentiment expressed in Proverbs:

"Let not mercy and truth forsake thee: bind them about thy neck; write them upon the table of thine heart." (Proverbs 3:3)

Clearly the purpose of binding the law about the neck and writing it on the heart is to reinforce obedience and to prevent us from forsaking mercy and truth. The purpose is not knowledge, but obedience.

Paul declares that it is the Holy Spirit who is the divine author of things written on the heart:

"Ye are our epistle written in our hearts, known and read of all men: Forasmuch as ye are manifestly declared to be the epistle of Christ ministered by us, written not with ink, but with the Spirit of the living God; not in tables of stone, but in fleshly tables of the heart." (2 Corinthians 3:2-3)

The third means of reinforcement at our disposal is the grace concentrated in the church. Though the church can distort the Law of God and become an agent of legalism, or so neglect the Law as to give license to sin, its divine vocation is to nurture our souls and assist in our progress toward sanctification.

The church is called "holy" because its vocation is holy—it is endowed with the presence of the Spirit—and because it is made up of people who are called "saints." The saints are so called not because they are perfect, but because they have been set apart by God and indwelt by the Holy Spirit.

The means of grace, which comes through the church and reinforces our desire to obey, includes the preaching of the Word by which we are comforted and exhorted. It also includes sacred worship, by which our souls are elevated in adoration and praise for God and through which we are reminded of the majesty of the One we are called to obey. The sacraments feed and nurture us in our Christian walk. Prayer brings us into regular communion with the One we seek to please, and through fellowship we enjoy the benefits of the mutual encouragement of the Christian community.

It is both foolish and wicked to suppose that we will make much progress in sanctification if we isolate ourselves from the visible church. Indeed, it is commonplace to hear people declare that they don't need to unite with a church to be a Christian. They claim that their devotion is personal and private, not institutional or corporate. This is not the testimony of the great saints of history; it is the confession of fools.

At times, circumstances keep people, through no fault of their own, cut off and isolated from the church. This happens, for example, to prisoners of war and those interned in concentration camps. It is an added burden to such people if they are isolated from fellow believers.

That Joseph, after being sold into slavery and exported to a pagan nation, remained so devoted to God makes his example of obedience all the more remarkable. Fortunately, God's Law was so strongly written in his heart that he was able to stand firm in the day of temptation.

Joseph not only kept faith with God through the episode with Potiphar's wife, but he also persevered to the end. He remained a model of obedience until his death. His faith is celebrated in the roll call of heroes in Hebrews 11:

"By faith Joseph, when he died, made mention of the departing of the children of Israel; and gave commandment concerning his bones." (Hebrews 11:22)

We could add to this praise that by faith Joseph remained chaste though assailed by the full force of erotic temptation. By faith he kept the Law and kept his soul from sinning grievously against God.

8

THE
SOUL AND
ITS VALUE

*W*HEN WE SPEAK OF THE DEPTHS of the human soul as the location of the Holy Spirit's work in us, and when we talk about the love of the Law of God that reaches us through divine illumination and grasps the soul, we become aware that the very concept of "soul" is assailed by doubt on the one hand and obscured by ambiguity on the other.

We wonder if it is even possible, in our day and age, to speak meaningfully about the human soul. In fact, there is little, if any, reason to speak of the human soul in our culture. The idea that an integral and essential aspect of our humanity survives death is highly suspect in modern worldviews. People in our culture tend to think of life in almost exclusively physical categories.

Yes, people still speak of concepts such as "mind" or the "self." But more and more the idea of "mind" is defined as a chemical-physical apparatus. And in some schools of thinking, thought itself is reduced to a series of "electrical" impulses that ultimately become physical responses. That thought and mind are non-physical realities is no longer taken for granted.

On the other hand, John Gerstner, author of *Reasons for Faith*, draws a sharp and *essential* distinction between mind and matter. When asked to distinguish the two, Gerstner quotes the puppet Punch. "What is Matter?—Never mind! What is Mind?—No matter!"[1]

In the seventeenth century, French philosopher and mathematician René Descartes probed the ageless question of the relationship between mind and body and between thought and action.[2] In his complex discussion of the interaction between the two, he was concerned with how thoughts give rise to actions and how actions give rise to thoughts.

At this moment in time I am engaged in the process of writing a book. My mind is focused on the ideas I want to put down on paper. Some of you, as you read, may wonder if I'm "out of my mind" altogether, yet all the while you are aware that you are reading thoughts coming from my mind. For me to get my thoughts from my head to your head, certain actions have to take place. The first action is that in which I am engaged. I have a pen in my hand, and I am putting words on paper. Later these words will be typed on a word processor. Still later they will be typeset, printed on pages, and published as a book. But for now it is an exercise in pen and ink. I am not consciously thinking about the physical action of manipulating the pen with my hand. (My secretary will attest to that after she tries to decipher my handwriting.) Again, the *focus* of my mind is on the thoughts I am writing. Yet without the function of my mind, I would not be able to guide this pen across the page at all, an action prompted and controlled by my mind. My fingers do not function independently from my brain. (Whoops! I just slipped into the modern view by identifying my mind with my brain.) This is the type of question Descartes probed. But there is another side to the action.

I just interrupted my writing to ask the waiter for some iced tea. (Howard Hughes once remarked that he had an office in every hotel in America because he had the eccentric habit of scheduling business meetings in the men's room. I have an office in every restaurant in America where I sit and write. Please keep that a secret lest I get charged rent by all these places.) Why did I go through the process of ordering iced tea? I was thirsty. The "action" of thirst provoked an idea in my mind. The idea was to have something to drink. I then translated that idea into action and ordered iced tea.

You too are engaged in an action with your body. You are reading this book. You are using your eyes to look at these words, or your ears to hear them if someone is reading them to you, or your fingers to feel them if you are reading them in braille. As you read, listen, or feel, the action produces thoughts in your own mind. Those thoughts will become actions if you give this book to a friend to read, or if you write a letter to me and tell me what you think of my ideas.

Thoughts generate actions and actions generate thoughts. Actions are basically physical. Thoughts are basically non-physical (though for now they seem to require a physical apparatus—i.e., a brain—to have them). Descartes distinguished body from mind by using the terms *extension* and *non-extension*.[3] The extended is that which takes up space and can be measured. The non-extended takes up no space and is immeasurable. Descartes borrowed from mathematics to discover a way to connect the two. He used the mathematical concept of the "point" to bridge the gap. The "point" is a philosophical hybrid, neither fish nor fowl. It takes up space but has no measurable extension.

Descartes' solution to the question of the relationship between thought and action was challenged by later thinkers who offered different theories to account for the interaction of the body and mind. No one, however, has been able to fully and finally avoid the essential difference between mind and body. Even those who argue that thoughts are nothing more than physical actions determined by uncontrollable physical causes use thoughts to try to persuade us of their viewpoint. If we are totally conditioned to think what we think, then the argument that we are so conditioned is likewise conditioned and has no logical validity. If all arguments are determined by physical causes, no argument can be valid, including the argument that all arguments are determined by physical causes. Such an argument would in fact be *mindless*.

In thinking about thought we cannot transcend thought itself. To contemplate thought we must think to do it. The very exercise involves an awareness of something non-physical.

Immanuel Kant is famous for his landmark work *The Critique of Pure Reason* in which he launched a massive criticism of the traditional arguments for the existence of God. He ended in theological agnosticism. In the process, Kant made a crucial distinction between two realms. He called these two realms the *noumenal* and the *phenomenal.*[4] The phenomenal realm, or world, is, as the word suggests, the realm of *phenomena.* This is basically the physical world that we encounter with our five senses. It is the realm that we can see, hear, taste, touch, or smell. It is the world of scientific inquiry, a realm that can be measured and analyzed by observation, experimentation, and the like. It is the sensible world, the world open to the senses.

We live in the post-Kantian nexus. The abiding question of philosophy today is this: Is there anything more? Is there a realm above, beyond, underneath, outside, or behind the sensible world? In addition to the sensible world or *physical* realm, is there a realm we call *meta*-physical? Kant argued that there may be such a realm, but if there is, we have no access to it. This extra-physical realm he called *noumenal.*

Theology has suffered from Kant's agnosticism and skepticism because he assigned God to the noumenal world. For Kant, if God exists he remains locked in a realm to which we have no access. Reason cannot rise to this realm nor can empirical science explore it. People can "leap" to it by faith, but such a leap is always non-scientific and/or mindless. Kant personally felt constrained to affirm the existence of God for practical reasons. He argued that we must live "as if" there were a God, because without that assumption, ethics would be meaningless, and without ethics society disintegrates. (He was certainly right about that. Dostoyevski went even further into that line of thinking. He wrote that without God *all* things are permissible.)

Though Kant retained the idea of God in his ethical and practical thinking, he remained agnostic about the ability to know God through theoretical thought.

This is not the place to respond to Kant's theoretical agnosticism regarding the existence of God. I've done that in *Classical Apologetics*. But it is important to see that part of the fallout from Kant's skepticism is the confusion about the reality and nature of the human soul. God is not the only entity or concept Kant assigned to the noumenal world. He also exiled two other vital concerns of traditional philosophy to this theoretical never-never land. These were (1) philosophical *essences* (things in themselves) and (2) the *self*.

The first of these we can leave to philosophers to debate. But the second is vital to our concern about the soul. Kant was as agnostic about knowing the self as he was about knowing God. And just as he made an end run to get to God via practical ethics, he did an end run to preserve some idea of the human self. Though he said that the self could not be known through conventional means of knowledge, he still affirmed it. Kant got to the self by what he called (in somewhat obscure language) the *transcendental apperception of the ego.*[5]

The layperson hears this phrase and justly asks, "What in the world is that?" Kant would scold us for making it a question of something "in the world" because doing so pulls it from the noumenal realm back into the phenomenal realm. If you asked Kant, "What in the world is that?" he would probably say, "It is nothing in the world, but it is still something."

I call the transcendental apperception of the ego an "end run" because it seeks to go around rational or scientific inquiry.

Kant based his affirmation of the self on "apperception," which is an awareness of something by some means other than "perception." To perceive something is to get in touch with it through one of the five senses. Kant understood that people cannot see, touch, hear, taste, or smell "self." But they can see, touch, hear, taste, and smell their *bodies.* Therefore, the body is not to be confused with the self.

Kant's way of thinking is a quasi-mystical, intuitive, or immediate awareness of the self. The crucial point is this: After all the philosophical and scientific analysis is said and done, we can't get away from the idea that we are aware of ourselves as selves. Perhaps there is nothing more foundational or primary to all reasoning than the simple reality of self-concious-ness. It is basic to human life itself. Though it may defy scientific analysis, it actually precedes scientific analysis and is the necessary pretheoretical condi-tion for scientific analysis.

I often play a little game with my students. I ask them two questions: "What is your name?" and "Where do you live?" If one says, "I live in Chi-cago," I then ask, "Are you now in Chicago?" After the student answers, "No, I'm in Orlando," I say, "Are you now alive?" With a bewildered expression the student says, "Of course." Then I say, "If you live in Chicago and you are not now in Chicago, how can you be alive?" Eventually I point out that what they mean by saying they "live" in Chicago is that their home or place of residence is in Chicago. Where they actually live is wherever they are at the moment. They live inside their bodies, so wherever their bodies are, they live. I live in my body, but the "I" that lives in my body cannot be reduced to my body.

If I lose a part of my body to amputation, "I" still exist. My "self" is still functioning.

If in an accident I become a paraplegic, I do not cease to exist. My legs may be paralyzed and my

activity severely restricted, but the self is still functioning.

We all are aware of a conscious interior life. We
may refer to it as our mind, consciousness, soul, or
spirit. Whatever we call it, we are aware that it
differs significantly from our bodies. It is in an
intimate relationship to our body, but it is not our
body.

MAN AS SUBSTANTIAL DICHOTOMY

Theology uses the term *substantial dichotomy* to refer
to the dual aspects of human composition. The
word *dichotomy* comes from a combination of Greek
words that mean "to cut in two." Unfortunately, we
often use the word *dichotomy* to refer to two different
and conflicting entities that cannot be resolved.
Some, therefore, reject the theological concept of
substantial dichotomy because it implies an irrecon-
cilable *dualism* that destroys the unity of human
existence.

However, that is not the meaning of the theological concept. The human makeup is not a dualism; it
is a *duality*. It is unity-in-duality. We are each *one*
person with two essential aspects, body and soul.

The earliest biblical reference to this idea is the
creation narrative:

"And the LORD God formed man of the dust of the ground, and breathed into his nostrils the breath of life; and man became a living soul." (Genesis 2:7)

In this graphic description man is created in two distinct stages. First the body is formed. But it is inanimate, inert, and lifeless. Not until God breathes the breath of life into it does it become a living soul. The language here does not say that man *gains* a living soul but that he *becomes* a living soul. This does not mean that the body becomes a soul or that the whole person is now only soul. He *is* a living soul precisely because he now *has* a soul.

Another passage from Genesis makes this clear:

"And it came to pass, as her soul was in departing, (for she died) that she called his name Ben-oni." (Genesis 35:18)

This speaks of the departure of the soul from the body. When the body dies, the soul continues in action. The same idea is communicated in 1 Kings 17:21:

"And he stretched himself upon the child three times, and cried unto the LORD, and said, O LORD my God, I pray thee, let this child's soul come into him again."

The soul inhabits the body. It comes from God to the body and at death departs from the body. The whole person then consists of body and soul. These are two distinct realities or "substances." Hence the concept of "substantial dichotomy."

TRICHOTOMY

Throughout church history various attempts have been made to deny the twofold nature of humanity and replace it with a threefold, or tripartite, view. This is attractive to some because of its analogous character to the nature of God. Since God is triune, some believe that beings created in God's image must also be triune. But fascination with the number three is hardly justification for such a view. If we pressed the analogy, we would have to conclude that we are three in the sense that God is three, namely in persons. God is triune but is by no means trichotomous. God is *one* in substance, not three.

A more frequent case for a tripartite view of humanity is drawn from biblical inferences. Two texts are generally cited to support this view. The first is from Paul's first epistle to the Thessalonians:

"And the very God of peace sanctify you wholly; and I pray God your whole spirit and soul and body be preserved blameless unto the coming of our Lord Jesus Christ." (1 Thessalonians 5:23)

Paul mentions three aspects of our humanity: spirit, soul, and body. Is the apostle revealing something about the makeup of humanity?

I think not. If we follow such logic, we could not stop at *three* substances but would have to add more. Elsewhere the Bible lists other distinct aspects of our humanity. Compare, for example, Mark 12:30:

"And thou shalt love the Lord thy God with all thy heart, and with all thy soul, and with all thy mind, and with all thy strength: this is the first commandment."

No one infers from this, the Great Commandment, that it reveals the constituent parts of man. We do not infer that we have a fourfold nature simply because the text mentions four aspects. Elsewhere the Scripture speaks of the will and the bowels. At times the terms *spirit* and *soul, heart* and *mind, mind* and *will* are used interchangeably. It is a dangerous business to read too much into this language.

Sometimes the Bible uses spirit and soul interchangeably, while at others it distinguishes them:

"For the word of God is quick, and powerful, and sharper than any twoedged sword, piercing even to the dividing asunder of soul and spirit, and of the joints and marrow, and is a discerner of the thoughts and intents of the heart." (Hebrews 4:12)

The effect of God's Word is so great that it can, in its piercing power, even divide soul and spirit. This may be a figurative and hyperbolic way of saying that God's Word can make distinctions we cannot make. It can divide asunder that which is by nature united.

The same text refers to the "thoughts of the heart." We usually think of the heart either as the seat of emotions or simply as a physical organ needed to pump blood through our bodies. Generally we associate thoughts with the mind. Here, however, the thoughts of the heart refer to the innermost thoughts we have. The heart is the core or central part of the person.

Historically the church has considered the distinctions of mind, heart, will, spirit, and soul to be *functional* distinctions, not essential or substantial distinctions. The notion of substantial dichotomy gets at the basic point: We have a physical dimension and a non-physical dimension to our lives. The term *body* incorporates all the parts and facets of the physical being, and the term *soul* incorporates all the facets of the non-physical, or spiritual, being.

THE DANGERS OF TRICHOTOMY

There is no horrible evil in viewing our human nature in trichotomous or tripartite terms. Many sound and orthodox Christians have adopted such a view. There is, however, a serious danger that lurks behind it, a danger that has caused the church historically to shy away from it.

The danger is this: Where trichotomy has been advanced and embraced, it was often "driven" by some prior heretical notion.

The heretic Apollinarius was condemned for his trichotomous view for two main reasons. The first was for his fracturing the human nature of Christ by saying that Jesus had a human body and a human soul, but he had a divine spirit. The second reason was because it appeared that he embraced a Greek view of body and soul that was likewise heretical.[6]

The Greek view was clearly one of *dualism*. It said that body and soul are intrinsically in conflict. Body is by nature evil, and soul is good. The only way they can coexist in a person is if the tension between body and soul can be bridged or relieved by a third substance, namely spirit. Here the spirit is conceived as a philosophical necessity to overcome the inherent dualism of humanity.

Since biblical Christianity flatly rejects such a

dualistic view, it also rejects the trichotomy that assumed it.

A similar danger lurks in the teaching of Watchman Nee, who has gained a wide following among evangelical Christians. Nee's work represents a synthesis between biblical teaching and oriental dualism. The dualism comes through in his view of trichotomy.

The charismatic movement has brought a widespread renewal of trichotomy. It uses this view to justify the baptism of the Holy Spirit, by which some believers have the Holy Spirit in their souls but not in their spirits, while others have the Holy Spirit in both. I can find absolutely no support for this in Scripture.

Modern dispensational theology follows a similar pattern in its doctrine of sanctification, which rests in part on its assumption of trichotomy. The Scofield Bible embraced the tripartite view. In a footnote to Genesis 1:26-27 we read:

> That man was made in the "image and likeness" of God. This "image" is found chiefly in man's tri-unity, and in his moral nature. Man is "spirit and soul and body" (1 Thes. 5.23). "Spirit" is that part of man which "knows" (1 Cor. 2.11), and which allies him to the spir-

itual creation and gives him God-consciousness. "Soul" in itself implies self-conscious life, as distinguished from plants, which have unconscious life.

In the dispensational view, people can be Christians but remain carnal. They have the Holy Spirit in their soul but not in their spirit. Only the Spirit-filled Christian has the Holy Spirit indwelling the human spirit. So there are two distinct classes of Christians: one carnal and the other spiritual.[7]

THE VALUE OF THE SOUL

Far more important than the theological discussion between dichotomy and trichotomy is the importance of the life of the soul. On at least one crucial point both sides clearly agree: Man has a soul. What remains to be seen is how valuable we regard the soul to be.

I hesitate to even use the term *value* in any discussion of theology due to the loose manner in which it is used in our culture. Often the words *values* and *value systems* are used in place of what used to be called ethics or even morals.

There is a subtle danger behind this apparently innocent change in language.

The term *value* connotes worth or importance. Historically it has been used to express matters of personal preference.

In the science of economics the phrase *subjective theory of value* is useful and important. The phrase itself has value. It communicates that "the value of goods and services is dependent upon the person seeking them." The value of a certain thing depends upon how much I desire it or esteem it. It is a matter of subjective preference. No one can tell me how much my car is worth to me. I can get an estimate of the market value of my home, but I cannot sell it until I find a person who values my home enough to purchase it from me. Some people value chocolate ice cream more than vanilla, but there is no absolute that says chocolate is *better* than vanilla.

When ethics are reduced to subjective values, laws become a matter of preference. There is no right or wrong, just preferences, or "values."

Yet value has an important place in the Kingdom of God. To seek the mind of Christ in spiritual sanctification involves in large measure an attempt to bring personal values in line with the values of Christ. Jesus himself used language borrowed from the economic world when he taught on the importance of the soul:

"For what is a man profited, if he shall gain the whole world, and lose his own soul? or what shall a man give in exchange for his soul?" (Matthew 16:26)

Jesus asked a "bottom-line" question and applied an eternal balance sheet to the relative worth of the human soul. He asked a question about net profit. What is left after we calculate income and expenses?

On the gain, or assets, side of Jesus' balance sheet we have one entry: the entire world. On the loss, or liability, side there is also only one thing recorded: the soul. According to the divine accounting system, this amounts to a net loss. In fact, we are eternally bankrupt.

Jesus is saying that neither something alone nor all goods and services added together are worth as much as one human soul. No earthly merchandise can be traded for a soul.

"What shall a man give in exchange for his soul?" is a rhetorical question. The obvious answer is "Nothing." We own nothing and can gain nothing of equal, or even near equal, value to our soul.

Our souls are far and away the most valuable possessions we have. We don't always assign such high value to the soul, however. It is cynically said that "Every man has his price." In other words, we are all willing to sell our souls if the price is right.

Winston Churchill is alleged to have said to his archenemy Lady Astor, "Would you be willing to go to bed with me for a million pounds?" Lady Astor looked at Churchill distastefully and replied, "Well, maybe, for a million pounds." Then Churchill quipped, "How about for ten shillings?" Lady Astor registered her disgust by replying, "Heavens no! What do you think I am?" Churchill answered, "Madame, we've already established what you are, we're just haggling over the price."[8]

This anecdote is funny, but spiritual prostitution is no laughing matter. Israel was repeatedly accused by God of playing the harlot for being unfaithful to their covenant. Likewise the church, the bride of Christ, can slip into harlotry by devaluing the worth of human souls.

We live in a market economy in which physicians are among the highest-paid professionals. Ministers, on the other hand, are among the lowest paid. We are willing to pay high sums of money for bodily care. Yet when it comes to the care and nurture of our souls we are niggardly.

In the national economy of Israel, God allowed the price of goods and services to be determined by the marketplace, but with one crucial exception. He required that every person pay a tithe, which was distributed to the Levites, who were entrusted with ministry and education. God took special steps to ensure the care and nurture of the soul. These steps are commonly ignored in modern culture.

Every year I teach doctor of ministry courses in the seminary. Students in this program must have served at least five years in the ministry to be eligible to enroll. When the pastors come together in this setting, they discuss matters in class that they would never discuss with their own congregations. There is no way I can overstate or exaggerate the severe financial difficulties these men face. None of them enter ministry for the sake of making money. They know they aren't going to get rich. But often they are deeply discouraged and wounded by the message they receive at salary time when they find out how little they and their work are worth to the people they care for.

I feel deeply for them. I try to encourage them and remind them that they are duty bound to value the souls entrusted to them even if those souls don't value them in return. The pastor must value his sheep more than the sheep value the shepherd or even themselves. This is precisely what Christ does for us.

Elsewhere Jesus spoke of the relative value of body and soul:

"And fear not them which kill the body, but are not able to kill the soul: but rather fear him which is able to destroy both soul and body in hell." (Matthew 10:28)

Again Jesus puts a premium on the value of the soul. The body may perish, but the soul lives on into eternity. To lose one's soul in hell is to suffer the eternal loss of our most precious possession.

To value the soul is to attend diligently to its nurture and growth that it might move from grace to grace and from life to life.

9

THE
FEEDING
OF THE SOUL

*I*F A SOUL IS TO BE NURTURED IT MUST be fed and given priority attention. This is the task of the church. Although God himself is the author and dispenser of the grace by which we are justified and sanctified, he has given to the church the means of grace.

God uses *means,* or *instruments,* to lead us into holiness. As a surgeon uses a scalpel and the physician uses medicine to effect a cure, so the curing of our sin-sick souls is administered by grace.

One of the vows I took when I became a communicant member of a church was "to make diligent use of the means of grace." Before I can make diligent use of anything I need to know what it is I am using. When I first made that vow, I had no idea what it meant—because I didn't know what the means of grace were.

THE MEANS OF GRACE

The first instrument by which sanctifying grace is dispersed to us is Scripture itself. As we have established, there is no hope of reaching a deeper level of Christian growth and experience if we neglect the Word of God.

When Paul brings both Jew and Gentile before the tribunal of God and convicts both of being under sin, he asks:

"What advantage then hath the Jew? or what profit is there of circumcision?" (Romans 3:1)

Paul answers his own question in emphatic terms:

"Much every way: chiefly, because that unto them were committed the oracles of God." (Romans 3:2)

Being a member of the commonwealth of Israel was no small advantage, as Paul indicates by the words, "Much every way." Then he indicates the *chief* of those advantages, namely the oracles or the Word of God.

If Israel had a redemptive advantage, members of the Christian church have an even greater advantage. To be a church member is no more a guarantee of salvation than was being a Jew in the Old Testament. But to be a church member is to be in a better position to receive grace because it is in the church that the means of grace are heavily concentrated. In this sense, at least, we can say with Augustine, "He who does not have the church as his mother does not have God as his Father."[1]

In the church we have the Word of God proclaimed. We also hear it *explained*, as the church has been given teachers equipped by God to help us understand and apply the Scripture to our lives. Though the Holy Spirit is the supreme teacher of God's Word, he is not the only teacher. Paul declares:

"Now ye are the body of Christ, and members in particular. And God hath set some in the church, first apostles, secondarily prophets, thirdly teachers, after that miracles, then gifts of healings, helps, governments, diversities of tongues." (1 Corinthians 12:27-28)

The teaching office of the church is instituted by God and given for our edification. We need teachers if we are to make diligent use of the means of grace, which includes the Word.

In his work *On Knowing Christ*, Jonathan Edwards writes, "There is no other way by which any means of grace whatsoever can be of any benefit, but by knowledge. Therefore the preaching of the Gospel would be wholly to no purpose if it conveyed no knowledge to the mind."[2]

Edwards, in pursuing his concern that we diligently inquire after the knowledge of God, says, "Therefore the acquisition of knowledge in these things should be a main business of all those who have the advantage of enjoying the Holy Scriptures."[3]

Edwards speaks of the truths of the Bible as being of "superlative excellency" and of "infinite importance" to all Christians. He adds:

> As to other sciences, he hath left us to ourselves, to the light of our own reason. But divine things being of infinitely greater importance to us, he hath not left us to an uncertain guide; but hath himself given us a revelation of the truth in these matters, and hath done very good things to convey and confirm it to us; raising up many prophets in different ages, immediately inspiring them with his Holy Spirit, and confirming their doctrine with innumerable miracles or wonderful works out of the established course of nature. Yea, he raised up a succession of prophets, which was upheld for several ages.[4]

Edwards concludes from his summary of God's revelatory activity that "If God doth such great things to *teach* us, we ought to do something to *learn.*"[5]

In the case of divine revelation, we cannot glibly remark that if the student didn't learn, it was because the teacher didn't teach. We cannot fault the teacher. If we continue in ignorance of the Word of God, the fault is ours. It involves a woeful negligence of this means of grace.

Persistence in such negligence does not reflect a mere weakness in the life of the Christian. Rather, it indicates that the professed believer is no believer at all. The person's profession of faith is spurious, and the Holy Spirit does not dwell in him or her.

Jesus himself declared:

"If ye continue in my word, then are ye my disciples indeed; and ye shall know the truth, and the truth shall make you free." (John 8:31-32)

This saying of Jesus is couched in conditional terms. It is an *if–then* statement. The stated "if" condition, which clearly calls us to "continue," or "remain," in his Word, is necessary for authentic discipleship. If we take this condition seriously, we must infer that its opposite is equally true, namely that if we do not continue in his Word, we are not his disciples. If we are not his disciples, we will not

be made free, and we will continue under the bondage of sin.

A disciple, or "student," of Christ is one who
enrolls for the whole course. There is no graduation
from this school until we enter heaven. True disciples do not merely dabble in Scripture or occasion-
ally allow their ears to be tickled by the Word of
God. True disciples are earnest and diligent in abiding in the Word.

WORSHIP AS A MEANS OF GRACE

The second means of grace by which we are spiritually strengthened is worship, which involves a posture of obeisance before the majesty of God and an
expression of unfeigned adoration springing from
the deepest chambers of the soul. Jesus said to the
Samaritan woman:

"But the hour cometh, and now is, when the true
worshippers shall worship the Father in spirit and in
truth: for the Father seeketh such to worship him."
(John 4:23)

The two requirements of acceptable worship are
that it be offered in a spiritual manner and that it be
according to truth. We can gain insight by consid-
ering their opposites. The opposite of spirit is flesh,

and the opposite of true is false. God finds carnal worship and false worship repugnant and unacceptable. Rather than please him, they offend his holiness and insult his honor.

Worship that is perfunctory or indifferent is carnal. Indeed, it is not worship at all. When we attend a service of worship but keep our spirits uninvolved, we dishonor the one who is worthy of worship.

As God is eternally and intrinsically worthy of our worship, it is our moral obligation to render it. Worship is God's due. We commit spiritual treason when we fail to give God his due. We commit the ultimate injustice. Failure to give proper worship to God is perhaps the most basic and egregious sin of the human race. This omission is the foundation for the universal indictment of mankind before the tribunal of God and the basis for the revelation of God's wrath against us. Paul belabors the point in Romans 1. He declares that men are left "without excuse" because

"When they knew God, they glorified him not as God, neither were thankful; but became vain in their imaginations, and their foolish heart was darkened. . . . [They] changed the truth of God into a lie, and worshipped and served the creature more than the Creator, who is blessed for ever." (vv. 21, 25)

The apostle focuses on three distinct violations of proper worship. The first is the refusal to glorify God as God. To "glorify" is to attribute "weight" or significance to God. It is to treat him with the respect he deserves. In a word it requires an attitude of *reverence*. When the Bible cites the fear of God as the starting point of all wisdom it is speaking not of a servile fear, such as a prisoner has for his torturer, but a reverential fear characterized by awe. God is altogether *awe*ful.

The reverse of glorifying God is taking him lightly. Scripture's emphasis on the manner in which the name of God is used is not grounded in some magical belief in incantations. Rather, the name of God is guarded as holy because the God whose name it is, is holy. How could it be possible to revere God while at the same time using God's holy name as a flippant curseword or a cavalier and thoughtless expression? The lips reveal the state of the heart.

When I was a boy I thought nothing of using my fists to punish anyone who insulted the good name of my mother, but I was unconcerned about the sanctity of the name of my heavenly Father. The reason was obvious: I revered my mother but had no reverence for God.

The second violation the apostle mentions is ingratitude. Since God is the author of every good and perfect gift, he deserves our everlasting gratitude. We owe him our very lives. To lack gratitude is an attitude of supreme arrogance. Ungratefulness indicates a heart so filled with pride and self-sufficiency that no room is left for gratitude.

True worship flows from a grateful heart. But again, the heart cannot be properly grateful unless or until the mind understands the reason for gratitude. Before our hearts can be duly moved to gratitude, we must be aware that the benefits of life flow to us from God's providence. To grow in gratitude requires that we first grow in our understanding of grace. As long as we entertain delusions of our own merit or compliment ourselves on our own contributions to salvation, we block our hearts from pure worship.

It is important for the Christian to realize and remember that these two violations of true worship—irreverence and ingratitude—are so basic to our fallen human nature, so universal in their human manifestation, and so ingrained by repeated practice, that even conversion does not automatically or instantly eradicate them.

The great Baptist theologian Roger Nicole once remarked in my hearing, "We are all Pelagian by nature." Pelagius, the arch-heretic of the fourth century, insisted that man can become righteous without the assistance of God's grace. The Pelagian error, either in full or in part, is a constant plague on the church. Pelagian tendencies affect us all and blind us to the marvels of divine grace. If we are to err in our theology, let us err on the side of grace rather than on the side of human pride.

Against Pelagius, Saint Augustine urged that we embrace the salvific formula *sola gratia*. He emphasized that redemption is not merely facilitated by grace, but rather it is accomplished by grace *alone*. It is not grace *along with* something else, but grace alone. Grace alone means unvarnished, unalloyed, pure and simple grace. Augustus Toplady expressed this sentiment in the popular hymn "Rock of Ages": "Nothing in my hand I bring, simply to the cross I cling." Toplady's "nothing" did not include a little "something."

The doctrines of grace inflame the heart to gratitude and fuel the souls of the great saints, such as Augustine, Aquinas, Luther, Calvin, and Edwards. These Titans differed with each other at various points of doctrine, but on the concept of *sola gratia* their voices were united.

It is the doctrines of grace, however, that are either ignored or despised in the modern evangelical church. The doctrines that inspired the original evangelical reformation are almost in eclipse in our day.

The third violation of worship the apostle mentions is the culmination and natural consequence of the other two: idolatry. Idolatry is a type of worship—worship of the flesh—but it is false worship.

The practice of idolatry is most insulting to God. People are not satisfied merely to withhold proper worship from God. They add insult to injury by giving the reverence and obeisance due God to things other than God.

The human penchant for idolatry is so strong that it manifests itself in a multitude of ways. Not even the stringency of the first two commandments of the Decalogue can totally restrain us from this evil. Calvin rightly declared that mankind is a *fabricum idolarum*, a veritable "idol factory."[6] We mass-produce idols to substitute for the true God.

The infection of idolatry is so deeply rooted in us that though we may flee from the crass and obvious idolatry of worshiping trees or statues, we still seek a substitute for the God who is. To worship God in truth means to worship him in the totality of his revealed character. When we strip God of his wrath, justice, holiness, or sovereignty, we commit idolatry. A God who is not sovereign is not the God of Scripture. At this point Karl Barth was right when he warned that even Christianity, if distorted, can degenerate into a religion of idolatry.[7]

Worship offered in spirit and in truth is worship that proceeds from a reverent and humble heart and is directed to the true God revealed in Scripture. Such worship feeds and strengthens our own souls; it does not nurture God. God does not need our worship. False worship will never injure God, but it is calamitous to us.

PRAYER AND WORSHIP

A third means of grace given to the church is the exercise of prayer, both private and corporate. To progress in a spiritual relationship with God requires that we develop deep communion with him. That communion is two-way. God speaks to us in his Word; we speak to him in prayer. Hearing the Word of God demands a response. That response includes, but is not limited to, action. It requires verbal expression. God both invites and commands us to speak to him.

Again, this command is not for God's benefit. He can survive without our fellowship. Nor does he require our input to know what is going on in our lives. He knows our words before we speak them, our thoughts before we think them, and our acts before we do them. Like worship, prayer is for our benefit. We are the ones who need intimate communion with God. Such communion is our highest experience of fellowship.

The pattern for worship established by God in Old Testament Israel stressed prayer. The functions of the tabernacle and the temple majored in prayer. Jesus confirmed this in his words of rebuke to the money changers in the temple. He said that his Father's house was to be a house of prayer.

Jesus' words may have a strange ring to modern Christians. We tend to think of the church building as a house of preaching or a house of human fellowship. To be sure, these functions are to take place in church, but we generally stress them to such a point that we obscure the role of prayer.

I still remember with some frustration the consternation I experienced as a young Christian. Before we were married my wife-to-be and I used to end our dates with a time of prayer together. In our hometown the only church open at night was the Roman Catholic Church. All the Protestant churches were locked. We would go into the Catholic church, bow together on the kneeling benches, and pray.

When I asked my pastor why our church was locked every night, he explained that it was to keep the insurance rates down. I suggested that he ask the Monsignor of the Catholic church where they got their insurance. To no avail. The church is still locked, and I am still frustrated.

My family is part of a new mission church in the Presbyterian Church in America. Until we can secure a building of our own, we are meeting in one owned by Seventh-day Adventists. This building comes equipped with kneeling benches in every pew. I love them. Kneelers are a small matter, but a meaningful one to me. I love to be on my knees when I pray. It seems a most appropriate posture. I am somewhat chagrined when visitors to our church complain about the kneelers because they are "too Catholic." If to kneel when we pray means that we are getting "too Catholic," the next time I kneel on them I shall pray that we get more so. The issue of the Reformation was not over kneeling to pray. Luther never protested that Rome was spending too much time on its knees.

Corporate prayer is also to be done in spirit and in truth. Prayer and worship may be distinguished, but never separated. Prayer is an integral and necessary part of true worship. It is the discipline of the saints.

Beyond corporate prayer there is the exercise of private and personal prayer. Since I have written extensively on this elsewhere, I will simply offer a brief summary of the vital ingredients of effective prayer. I like the simple acrostic A-C-T-S as a tool to follow in prayer. The acrostic spells out the four main elements of prayer: Adoration—Confession—Thanksgiving—Supplication.

So often our prayer time is truncated and one-dimensional. We tend to spend most or all of our time engaged in supplication, which is to bring our petitions before God and entreat him to fulfill our personal requests and answer our particular needs and wants.

There is nothing wrong with supplication. It is a vital and necessary part of the sweet communion of prayer. Yet when we eavesdrop on the prayers of the great saints, we hear them putting great stress on the other elements as well. Adoration is not merely a brief preface or introduction to prayer, it is the very heart of it.

When the soul is moved to adoration it is usually because the mind has been contemplating the excellence of God. Such contemplation has a dual effect. First, it excites adoration. However, as we contemplate and adore the riches of God, we cannot help but be aware of the stark contrast between the fullness of his excellency and the corresponding lack of it in ourselves. Such awareness leads us inexorably from adoration to confession.

Adoration of God, like the Law of God, acts as a mirror to show us the blemishes of our character and drive us to a posture of contrition. Adoration includes obeisance, and obeisance is never genuine unless it proceeds from a humble heart.

The progression continues to the expression of thanksgiving. There is no benefit for which the Christian is moved to greater gratitude than that of God's divine pardon. In response to our confession, the Spirit comforts us and grants assurance that we are forgiven. Who is so hard of heart as to receive the pardon of God without wanting to scream to heaven, "Thank you!"

These elements—adoration, confession, and thanksgiving—combine to prepare our hearts for making supplications to him in a right and godly spirit.

FELLOWSHIP AS A MEANS OF GRACE

A fourth means of grace is fellowship. I am not speaking so much of the fellowship we enjoy with God, but of the fellowship the creed calls the "communion of the saints." Fellowship includes the sheer fun of friendship, but so much more is involved. As people together in the body of Christ, we are to encourage, comfort, and exhort one another. We rejoice with those who rejoice and weep with those who weep.

Mutual encouragement is a vital ingredient of fellowship. Encouragement, as the word suggests, helps to impart courage to the fainthearted. Cowardliness can be contagious, as sudden flights from enemies in battle indicate. But courage can also be contagious. The example of one courageous brother or sister can put steel in the hearts of the whole congregation.

The Christian life was never meant to be lived in isolation. When Christ redeems us he places us in a body of believers. I once heard a minister use an analogy of a barbecue grill and a mound of glowing pieces of charcoal. What happens, he asked, if you remove one of the burning coals from the heap and set it aside by itself? It soon ceases to glow and its warmth dissipates. So too the Christian who removes himself or herself from the fellowship of the saints loses the benefits of this vital means of grace.

SACRAMENTS, LITURGY, MUSIC, AND ARCHITECTURE

Though Christianity is established upon verbal revelation, it is enhanced by sacramental and liturgical exercises. The sacraments are visible signs that confirm to our senses the truth of the Word of God. The signs themselves are nonverbal, but they signify things that God has indeed verbalized.

The sacraments dramatize the Word of God. They involve actions that enhance communication.

Through the sign of baptism we are comforted by the assurance that God has placed his mark of ownership upon our souls, a mark that is indelible. Nothing can erase it. It is a sure and certain sign of God's promise to redeem those who believe. The validity of this sign rests not upon the minister who administers it or the person who receives it. It rests upon the integrity of the God who promises it.

As baptism seals the promises of God to our souls, so the Lord's Supper regularly and repeatedly nourishes and strengthens our souls. The Lord's Supper promises the grace-giving, real presence of Christ, who invites his people to his table for intimate fellowship with him.

The full import of the Lord's Supper is worthy of a volume all its own. Here I am compelled to pass over lightly what I can never take lightly. The older I get and the more I progress in faith, the more important this sacrament becomes to me. If there is any place I experience the mystic sweet communion of my soul with Christ, it is at his sacred table.

In one sense the experience of Holy Communion has become a source of embarrassment to me. I often find it necessary when communing to cover my eyes with my hands to shield from public view the tears I cannot stem. Indeed, the sweetness of such communion is at times almost more than I can bear as the profusion of Christ's presence floods my soul.

Our worship and sacramental devotion is regularly punctuated by the hearing and singing of sacred music. Music itself is a profound mystery to me. Secular anthropologists point to human speech in all of its complexity as a distinguishing characteristic of the human "animal." Cows moo, lions roar, and turkeys gobble their own kind of "speech," but nothing in the animal kingdom remotely resembles the complexity of human verbal communication.

When we add to the human capacity for speech the phenomenon of song, we enter into a new dimension of communication. Rhythm, harmony, tone, and poetic meter added to speech create a completely different form of communication which increases the depth of human expression. Song is a gift, a divine bonus by which we express our praise for God.

How God has marvelously gifted his church with the singular beauty of the works of Handel, Bach, and Mendelssohn. The great hymns of history stir our souls and inspire our spirits. An adoring church is a singing church as we lift our voices to glorify God.

Music adds a crucial dimension to spiritual worship—the dimension of beauty, a virtue itself grounded in the character of God. God is the fountainhead of all truth. All that is true circles back to bear witness to its ultimate source. God is the fountainhead of all goodness. Everything that is good reflects the virtue of its original Author. God is the fountainhead of all beauty. Everything that is beautiful displays the order, form, harmony, and proportionality that marks the Creator. This triad of virtues—the true, the good, and the beautiful—together comprise a unified witness to the Lord of Glory.

Poetry in song or in speech captures an element of expression that transcends ordinary language. The philosopher speaks to the mind, while the poet addresses the soul. It is a thing sublime that poetry added to music can lift our hearts and exalt our spirits to uncharted heights of praise.

Songs in the Bible generally mark a victory achieved by God for his people. When God redeemed his people from bondage in Egypt, Moses and Miriam vocalized their praise. When God routed the forces of Sisera, Deborah marked the event with an anthem of praise:

"Hear, O ye kings; give ear, O ye princes; I, even I, will sing unto the LORD; I will sing praise to the LORD God of Israel." (Judges 5:3)

The Annunciation of the birth of Jesus was marked by Mary's song, the Magnificat. Simeon sang the Nunc Dimittis and Zacharias the Benedictus. In heaven God promises his people a new song that we will sing to commemorate his final victory on our behalf.

The modern church is experiencing a crisis of worship. All sorts of experimental architectural forms dot the landscape as churches scramble to gain members and attract people to their programs. Buildings seem more and more to stress fellowship over the priority of worship. Gone are the vaulted ceilings and soaring arches of the past that expressed the transcendence of God. In the past the entrance to the church building was considered a threshold from the secular to the sacred, from the profane to the holy. That transition has been all but lost as our church buildings more and more resemble civic meeting houses.

The departure from classic structure and form is partly motivated by a reaction against liturgicalism, formalism, ritualism, and externalism. Zeal for authentic worship that does not lapse into empty ritual fuels this rejection of past form.

The prophets of Israel certainly voiced God's judgment against the degenerate dead formalism that emerged in history. Yet the prophets did not attack the forms themselves.

All worship has form. There is ritual in every church. Corporate worship is impossible without these things. The only real alternative to form is formlessness, which is chaos. God is not a God of chaos.

Our need is not for formlessness. We need forms, structures, and rituals that are biblically sound and conducive to worship. Liturgy can be an exercise in fatal formalism. It can also be a means of grace if grounded in the Word and practiced from the heart.

We need to think deeply about the forms and structures we use in worship. They matter deeply. They set the tone and ambience, the setting for worship. When good forms are used in a good manner, they promote worship as a means of grace and as a taste of heaven.

10

BARRIERS
TO PROGRESS

*I*N OUR LIFELONG QUEST FOR THE living god, we are pilgrims in a strange land. Like Abraham, the father of the faithful, we seek a better country whose builder and maker is God. We have not yet arrived at our destination. We encounter detours and roadblocks along the way. Sometimes our pilgrimage resembles the wilderness wanderings of the Israelites, whose route to the Promised Land was circuitous rather than direct. We are equipped with an impeccable map, but like proud husbands, we hate to admit we can't always decipher it, and so we refuse to ask directions when we lose our bearings.

We are seekers—seekers of God. We may adorn our bumpers with a bold sticker proclaiming that we have Found It, but what we have found is not our final destination. By finding Christ we have found the route to our final destination, but there is much traveling yet ahead. We are both finders and seekers, having found our Lord only to begin our search in earnest.

No unbeliever ever seeks God. The Bible avers that no one seeks after God (Romans 3:11). Popular theology tends to dispute this clear biblical teaching, however. Christian jargon is replete with expressions such as, "He is not a Christian, but he is searching for God." Such expressions flatly contradict the Word of God. No pagan ever seeks God.

Yet from our vantage point it often seems to us that unregenerate people are in fact seeking after God. But God is not hiding. He is in plain view. His creation clearly and manifestly displays his glory. Fallen humans are not by nature seekers after God. We are fugitives from God, fully intent upon escaping from him. Why then do we think unbelievers are searching for him?

Saint Thomas Aquinas offered a cogent answer to this question. He explained that the unbeliever desperately seeks happiness, peace of mind, meaning and significance in life, relief from guilt, and a host of other things we link inseparably with God. We make the gratuitous assumption that because people are seeking things that only God can give them that they are therefore seeking God. On the contrary, people seek the *benefits* of God, while all the while fleeing from God himself.

The dilemma is similar to another human phenomenon. Few, if any, would deliberately choose to go to hell. Permanent residence there is not a natural desire. We do not desire hell, but we do desire evil. The problem is that hell is the appointed consequence of evil. We desire evil without hell and heaven without God. This is the quintessential fool's errand. The pursuit of evil is the road to hell. The pursuit of God is the road to heaven.

To seek God is the business of the Christian. The quest *begins* at conversion; it doesn't end there. Once we have "found" him, the real search begins. We say "I found it" because he found us and now invites us to seek him until we pass through the veil into heaven.

Perhaps better than anyone, John Bunyan expressed the quest for God that marks the Christian life. *Pilgrim's Progress* is the allegorical story of a man who, in a dream, meets a man named Evangelist who asks the despondent hero why he is crying. His answer is poignant:

> Sir, I perceive by the Book in my hand, that I am condemned to die, and after that to come to

Judgment; and I find that I am not willing to do the first, nor able to do the second.[1]

The hero suffers from two problems. The first is a lack of willingness. He is unwilling to die. Like Shakespeare's Hamlet, he would rather bear those ills he has than fly to others he knows not of. Like the dilemma expressed in the song "Ole Man River," he is "tired of living, but scared of dying."

The second problem is one of inability. He lacks the ability to face the judgment of God. The expression is elliptical. What is tacitly assumed is not the inability to appear at judgment—that is inevitable—but to *survive* the judgment of God. He verbalizes his fear by saying:

I fear that this Burden that is upon my back, will sink me lower than the grave.[2]

The place "lower than the grave" is the abyss of hell. Like a fishing line with a small piece of lead attached at the end to make it sink to the depth of the lake, so the person weighted down by a massive burden of sin will sink into the depths of hell.

Christian, the hero of Bunyan's story, flees from the wrath to come, and sets his face toward the shining

Light and the Wicket Gate to seek an inheritance that
is incorruptible, undefiled, and which fades not away.
His course toward glory is marked by obstacles,
however. Friends named Obstinate and Pliable
mock him and try to dissuade him from his mission.
He encounters the slough of Despond early in his
pilgrimage and falls into it. A man named Help
rescues him from his plight and says:

> This miry slough is such a place as cannot be
> mended: It is the descent whither the scum and
> filth that attends Conviction for Sin doth con-
> tinually run, and therefore it is called the
> slough of Despond; for still as the Sinner is
> awakened about his lost condition, there
> ariseth in his soul many fears and doubts, and
> discouraging apprehensions, which all of them
> get together, and settle in this place: And this is
> the reason of the badness of this place.[3]

What Christian has never visited the slough of
Despond? Who has never tried to avoid it altogether?
Our souls have all been assailed by doubts, fears, and
discouragements. It is not by accident that the most
frequent admonition from the lips of Jesus in the
New Testament is the exhortation to "Fear not." All
of the counsel of the Mr. Worldly Wisemen of this

age cannot get us past this Slough. It requires the full assurance of our salvation to get us safely through.

THE ASSURANCE OF SALVATION

Perhaps nothing is more important to hasten us on the way to Christian maturity than a sound and solid assurance of salvation. When we are uncertain about our status in the kingdom, we are vulnerable to every fiery dart of Satan. We are reeds shaken in the wind. We become like corks in the sea, bobbing this way and that with each change of tide.

Stability is the mark of the mature Christian. Such stability is not possible, however, if the believer's foundation itself is not solid. Stable houses rest on stable foundations. The psalmist asks:

"If the foundations be destroyed, what can the righteous do?" (Psalm 11:3)

Jesus warned of the perils of a faulty foundation in his parable of the house built upon a rock:

"Whosoever cometh to me, and heareth my sayings, and doeth them, I will show you to whom he is like: He is like a man which built a house, and digged deep, and laid the foundation on a rock: and when the flood arose, the stream beat vehemently upon that house, and could not shake it; for it was founded upon a rock. But he that heareth, and doeth not, is like a man that without a foundation built a house upon the earth; against which the stream did beat vehemently, and immediately it fell; and the ruin of that house was great." (Luke 6:47-49)

Hearing this parable makes me wonder if Jesus was thinking of the contrast between the first two kings of Israel, Saul and David. Saul was a model of instability. When he and his empire crashed and Saul died in ignomy, David sang a poignant lament:

"The beauty of Israel is slain upon thy high places: *how are the mighty fallen!* Tell it not in Gath, publish it not in the streets of Askelon; lest the daughters of the Philistines rejoice, lest the daughters of the uncircumcised triumph. . . . *How are the mighty fallen* in the midst of the battle! O Jonathan, thou wast slain in thine high places. . . . *How are the mighty fallen*, and the weapons of war perished!" (2 Samuel 1:19-20, 25, 27)

By contrast, despite his dreadful fall into sin with Bathsheba, David reflected the man of Psalm 1:

"Blessed is the man that walketh not in the counsel of the ungodly, nor standeth in the way of sinners, nor sitteth in the seat of the scornful. But his delight is in the law of the LORD; and in his law doth he meditate day and night. And he shall be like a tree planted by the rivers of water, that bringeth forth his fruit in his season; his leaf also shall not wither; and whatsoever he doeth shall prosper. The ungodly are not so: but are like the chaff which the wind driveth away." (vv. 1-4)

In the parable of the house built upon a rock, there are two comparisons with Psalm 1. The first has to do with *hearing*. The person whose house is built upon the solid foundation of the rock is the one who "heareth my sayings, and doeth them."

G. C. Berkouwer, one of my professors in graduate school, was once honored by the publication of a scholarly *Festschrift*, which is a series of essays written by noted academicians in celebration of some milestone in the career of an outstanding professor. What struck me about the *Festschrift* honoring Berkouwer was not so much the content of the essays themselves as the title of the volume: *Ex Auditu Verbi*. In English the title means *Out of the Hearing of the Word*.

It is from hearing (and doing) the Word that the stable foundation is established. In like manner, the psalmist speaks of the man who does not walk in the counsel of the ungodly nor listen to the advice of

Mr. Worldly Wiseman, but who delights in the law of the Lord.

The second similarity between the parable and the psalm is the *depth* accented by both. Jesus spoke of a man who dug deep. His foundation went well beneath the surface. It is by digging deeply in the Word that we establish the sure foundation of assurance. The psalmist described the man who meditates on the Law day and night. Again, this is not a cursory reading of the Word. It is a serious, earnest, persistent study of the Word of God.

The person who digs deeply, who meditates day and night, is likened to a tree planted by the water. Its roots go deep; so deep that the tree is nourished sufficiently to bring forth fruit at the appropriate time. It is able to survive the severe, arid winds of the desert. Its leaf never withers in the scorched air. The blasts on the surface are withstood because the roots reach the water.

The water our souls require for survival is the assurance of salvation. This assurance does not always come immediately upon conversion. Indeed, in some cases it may remain elusive. Yet the gaining of full assurance is not only a spiritual privilege for the Christian, it is also a duty:

"Brethren, give diligence to make your calling and election sure: for if ye do these things, ye shall never fall." (2 Peter 1:10)

This divine mandate is set in a context of an exhortation to the bearing of spiritual fruit and virtue. Let us examine the broader context:

"According as his divine power hath given unto us all things that pertain unto life and godliness, through the knowledge of him that hath called us to glory and virtue: Whereby are given unto us exceeding great and precious promises: that by these ye might be partakers of the divine nature, having escaped the corruption that is in the world through lust. And beside this, giving all diligence, add to your faith virtue; and to virtue, knowledge; And to knowledge, temperance; and to temperance, patience; and to patience, godliness; And to godliness, brotherly kindness; and to brotherly kindness, charity. For if these things be in you, and abound, they make you that ye shall neither be barren nor unfruitful in the knowledge of our Lord Jesus Christ. But he that lacketh these things is blind, and cannot see afar off, and hath forgotten that he was purged from his old sins." (2 Peter 1:3-9)

Peter's listing of the fruit of the Holy Spirit corresponds remarkably with the listing provided by Paul in Galatians. The accent is upon the manifestation of the virtues associated with godliness. Peter speaks of the "exceeding great and precious promises" of God. These promises are given for a specific purpose: that we might partake of the Spirit and yield his fruit.

The key is found in verse 10, which promises that if we give diligence to making our calling and election sure, we will not fall.

The acquiring of a sound and certain assurance of salvation is vital to the full production of spiritual virtue. I use the phrase *sound assurance* because of the clear and present danger of "unsound," or false, assurance. As we will see, false assurance is a deadly error that some make.

The difficulty with gaining assurance of salvation is that it is possible to be unsaved and yet be fully assured that we are saved. Since it is possible both to be saved and know that we are saved, and to be unsaved and be sure that we are saved, how can we know in which category we truly are? How can we properly distinguish between false assurance and genuine assurance?

FALSE ASSURANCE OF SALVATION

False assurance of salvation is usually predicated on one of two fatal errors. The first is a false understanding of the conditions, or requirements, of salvation itself. The second is a false appraisal as to whether we have met the true requirements. The first is a faulty analysis of salvation; the second is a faulty analysis of ourselves.

False Views of Salvation

False views of salvation abound. For example, universalism teaches that Christ secured the salvation of all mankind. If indeed all human beings are saved, it is a small and logical step to conclude that all we have to be sure of is whether we are a member of the human race.

A second false view of salvation is based on a doctrine of justification by works. According to this doctrine, which is slightly more subtle than universalism, people assume that if they live a good life, or at least a "good enough" life, they will be saved.

This view involves a twofold error. The first error is that it denies the doctrine of justification by faith alone. It either eliminates faith as the sole necessity for justification or mixes works with faith as the foundation for salvation.

The second error contained in this view is one of self-appraisal. It assumes that a person's works are truly good or good enough to satisfy the demands of God's justice. But God's Law requires perfection, which no human being apart from Christ can achieve. It is because Jesus was sinless and we are sinful, because he was perfectly obedient and we are disobedient, that we must receive by faith his righteousness, his merit, to be saved.

The third false view of salvation is closely linked to the second. It assumes salvation by virtue of church membership—that those who are baptized and enrolled in a church may assume they are in a state of salvation. This presupposes that a mere profession of faith is sufficient for salvation and ignores the teaching of Christ that the visible church contains tares along with wheat, goats along with the true sheep. Jesus acknowledged that people are capable of honoring him with their lips while their hearts are far from him.

The fourth view assumes that the only requirement for salvation is to be "religious." If a person adheres to some religion, any religion, it is assumed the person is saved. This denies the exclusive role of Christ as the way to salvation, the only name under heaven by which we may be saved. The Bible makes it clear that pagan or idolatrous religion is repugnant to God. To be zealous in, for example, the religion of Baal was to magnify one's guilt before God, not to minimize it.

Faulty Self-Analysis

The second fatal error that yields a false assurance of salvation is a faulty self-analysis. If we understand the way of salvation and have a sound understanding of justification by faith alone, we may still delude ourselves regarding the question of whether we actually have saving faith.

How do we know if our faith is authentic? There are two basic tests for genuine faith. The first is an analysis of our own inner disposition. A regenerate person has received the internal operation of the Holy Spirit, by which the inclination or disposition of the soul has been changed. The regenerate heart has a love and desire for Christ that is not found in the unbeliever.

How do we know whether we love Christ? We may delude ourselves into thinking we love God or Christ when what we love is a false idol of our own making. There are numerous false portraits of Christ. The Antichrist is so-called not only because he sets himself *against* Christ but because he seeks to function as a *substitute* for Christ. He is a clever counterfeit designed to deceive people.

Given the human propensity toward idolatry, we must ask ourselves, Do we love the *biblical* Christ? Do we love the *biblical* God? It is easy to love a God stripped of holiness, wrath, justice, or sovereignty. If we recoil in horror at the biblical revelation of the character of God (given that we have a sound understanding of it), it indicates that the true God is not really an object of our affection.

One of the struggles of the true Christian is precisely at this point of subjective analysis. When we sin we become vulnerable to Satan's accusation. Satan knows full well that to attack our assurance is to threaten us with spiritual paralysis. When we sin Satan encourages us to ask ourselves, *How could I truly love Christ and do this?* The answer, of course, may be that we don't truly love Christ, in which case we do not have saving faith. On the other hand, a person can have saving faith and not love Christ perfectly. The question then becomes, Do I love Christ at all? To love the biblical Christ at all, a person must be regenerate. To know this I must know the biblical Christ. If faith comes by hearing and hearing by the Word of God, likewise assurance comes by hearing the Word of God. As I meditate on the Scriptures, my assurance is strengthened.

In addition to the question of the disposition of the heart, we must face the question of the presence or absence of the fruit of faith. Again, it is not a question of whether our fruit is perfect, but whether there is any fruit at all. No fruit means no faith. Some fruit means some faith. The Bible tells us we will know them by their fruit.

The fruit we are looking for is the fruit of obedience. Jesus taught that we show our love for him by keeping his commandments:

"He that hath my commandments, and keepeth them, he it is that loveth me: and he that loveth me shall be loved of my Father, and I will love him, and will manifest myself to him. . . . If a man love me, he will keep my words: and my Father will love him, and we will come unto him, and make our abode with him. He that loveth me not keepeth not my sayings: and the word which ye hear is not mine, but the Father's which sent me." (John 14:21, 23-24)

This is where works fit into the Christian life. We are not justified *by* our works, but we are justified *unto* works. The indispensable evidence of true faith is the presence of works. The works add nothing to the merit of Christ, by whose merit we are justified. But faith inevitably and necessarily produces works or it is not saving faith.

This is the point stressed by the apostle James, who asks the crucial question:

"What doth it profit, my brethren, though a man say he hath faith, and have not works? can faith save him?" (James 2:14)

James's obvious answer is that such "faith" is not saving faith. It is a dead faith, a spurious faith. James issues a challenge:

"Show me thy faith without thy works, and I will show thee my faith by my works." (James 2:18)

Faith is *shown* or demonstrated by works. If no works are demonstrated, saving faith is absent. To have assurance of salvation, we need objective evidence of fruit in our lives. A regenerate person is a changed person. Two vital changes have taken place. The first change is the disposition of the soul affected by the Holy Spirit. The second change is the indwelling of the Spirit.

If a person goes through two such alterations—regeneration and indwelling—it is simply impossible that there be no change in the individual's life. It is a root change, so radical that it is called a new creation. The change in the root produces change in the fruit.

Perhaps the most frightening warning Jesus ever gave regarding the perils of a false profession of faith is found in the conclusion of the Sermon on the Mount:

"Not every one that saith unto me, Lord, Lord, shall enter into the kingdom of heaven; but he that doeth the will of my Father which is in heaven. Many will say to me in that day, Lord, Lord, have we not prophesied in thy name? and in thy name have cast out devils? and in thy name done many wonderful works? And then will I profess unto them, I never knew you: depart from me, ye that work iniquity." (Matthew 7:21-23)

Jesus made use of a literary form that is rare in Scripture and consequently easy to overlook. He twice portrayed a person who comes to him and addresses him by the replication of the title Lord. The person does not merely say, "Lord, have I not . . . ". He says, "Lord, Lord."

Why the repeated use of the title Lord? To understand the full import of this address, we will make a brief reconnaissance through Scripture. The use of repetition in personal address occurs about fifteen times, certainly less than twenty times, in all of Scripture. Following are some examples.

When Abraham was put to the test by God and sent to Mt. Moriah to offer his son, Isaac, upon the altar, he was interrupted at the last second by the angel of the Lord. The angel called to him from heaven:

"*Abraham, Abraham:* and he said, Here am I. And he said, Lay not thine hand upon the lad, neither do thou any thing unto him: for now I know that thou fearest God, seeing thou hast not withheld thy son, thine only son from me." (Genesis 22:11-12)

When Jacob, advanced in years, was fearful of moving to Egypt, God spoke to him in a night vision:

"*Jacob, Jacob.* And he said, Here am I. And he said, I am God, the God of thy father: fear not to go down into Egypt; for I will there make of thee a great nation." (Genesis 46:2-3)

When Moses was living in exile in the Midianite wilderness, God spoke to him from the burning bush:

"*Moses, Moses.* And he said, Here am I. And he said, Draw not nigh hither: put off thy shoes from off thy feet; for the place whereon thou standest is holy ground." (Exodus 3:4-5)

At the end of the period of the judges when the boy Samuel ministered to Eli in the sanctuary, God spoke to him at night:

"*Samuel, Samuel.* Then Samuel answered, Speak; for thy servant heareth." (1 Samuel 3:10)

What was perhaps David's darkest hour came when he received the news of Absalom's death and uttered this poignant lament:

"O my son *Absalom, O Absalom, my son, my son!*" (2 Samuel 19:4)

Later, in the prophetic era, when Elijah reached the end of his life, he was accompanied by his student, Elisha, to the place of his translation into heaven. Upon watching Elijah be taken away, Elisha cried:

"*My father, my father,* the chariot of Israel, and the horsemen thereof. And he saw him no more. And he took hold of his own clothes, and rent them in two pieces." (2 Kings 2:12)

This strange form of duplicated address is also found in the New Testament. When Jesus visited the home of Mary and Martha in Bethany and Martha complained about her chores, Jesus said to her:

"*Martha, Martha,* thou art careful and troubled about many things: But one thing is needful; and Mary hath chosen that good part, which shall not be taken away from her." (Luke 10:41-42)

Likewise, when Jesus reproved Peter he said to him:

"*Simon, Simon,* behold, Satan hath desired to have you, that he may sift you as wheat: But I have prayed for thee, that thy faith fail not: and when thou art converted, strengthen thy brethren." (Luke 22:31-32)

Jesus' lament over Jerusalem assumes the same form:

"O *Jerusalem, Jerusalem*, which killest the prophets, and stonest them that are sent unto thee; how often would I have gathered thy children together, as a hen doth gather her brood under her wings, and ye would not!" (Luke 13:34)

In the midst of his agony on the cross, Jesus cried out to the Father:

"*Eli, Eli*, lama sabachthani? that is to say, *My God, my God*, why hast thou forsaken me?" (Matthew 27:46)

Finally, when Saul of Tarsus was converted on the road to Damascus, he was confronted by a voice from heaven calling to him:

"*Saul, Saul*, why persecutest thou me? And he said, Who art thou, Lord? And the Lord said, I am Jesus whom thou persecutest: it is hard for thee to kick against the pricks." (Acts 9:4-5)

This miniature survey reveals a clear pattern. In general the presence of repetition in Hebrew literature is a sign of emphasis. When the repetition involves personal address, it indicates a form of personal intimacy.

When Jesus warned that some people who call him "Lord, Lord" will not enter heaven, he was implying that they would be people who believed they had an intimate relationship with him. The warning is all the more alarming in that he said there will be "many" who will approach him in this manner. Indeed their claim will be insistent. They will appeal to their works as evidence of the authenticity of their personal relationship with Christ. They will include preachers, exorcists, and those who point to "wonderful works" they have done.

Yet despite these protests, they will be turned away. They will hear the most dreadful words human ears can ever hear from the lips of Christ. He will say to them, "Depart from me" and then declare that he *never* knew them.

These are not people who were once truly intimate with Christ who then fell away. They never belonged to him. They were never in a state of grace.

Why are these false professors sent away at the last day? Because they are workers of iniquity. Other translations say they are *lawless*.

The point of Jesus' solemn warning is as simple as

it is terrifying. It is not the person who professes faith who is saved; it is the one who does the will of the Father.

Works that are evidence of true faith are not merely activities of the church or ministry; they are works of obedience. We can be engaged in church or religious activities for all sorts of evil motives. Such works, even when God makes good use of them, do not please him. What pleases him is a genuine spirit of obedience, which is the fruit of genuine faith.

THE WITNESS OF THE SPIRIT

The final test for authentic assurance of salvation is the presence of the internal witness of the Holy Spirit. The apostle Paul wrote:

"For ye have not received the spirit of bondage again to fear; but ye have received the Spirit of adoption, whereby we cry, Abba, Father. The Spirit itself beareth witness with our spirit, that we are the children of God." (Romans 8:15-16)

Here the hungry soul finds nurture and the weary soul a resting place. It is the Holy Spirit himself who provides our final assurance by which we call God "Father" with confidence. This assurance comes with the Word and through the Word.

Once assured that he knows us and that we are truly his, we are equipped to continue our pilgrimage without fear of paralysis or final fall. Our destination is in sight, and our final goal is attainable.

11

THE SOUL'S
FINAL
DESTINATION

*I*T IS THE LOT OF MANKIND TO BE EVER engaged in the pursuit of happiness. Americans perceive this quest not only as a constitutional right, but as an inalienable right given by divine Providence. The government may be able to guarantee by law the right to pursue happiness, but no government can guarantee the *attainment* of happiness.

Happiness is elusive. To taste it is one thing; to hold it in our grasp is another. Our happiest moments in this world are at best fleeting. They are often bittersweet, rarely living up to expectations and always attended by the threat of loss.

The athletic arena is an example of our quest for joy. In a contest there is a winner and a loser. The loser suffers dejection while the winner experiences elation, but only until a new game or a new season begins, returning them to the starting line to begin the quest again. The golf professional who achieves his life's dream of winning the U.S. Open is hounded at the awards ceremony by reporters asking, "How do you think you'll do in the British Open?" Mario Lemieux, holding the Stanley Cup aloft, skates around the rink in a victory lap, only to face a new season plagued by crippling inquiries. Mike Tyson, the youngest man ever to win the heavyweight championship of the world, goes from winner to loser when he is convicted of rape and sentenced to prison.

What we want is not temporary happiness; we ache for a happiness that is permanent. Such is the quest of the soul, the destiny for which we were created.

The word *happiness* itself has become mongrelized, being mixed together with confusing emotions. What exactly is it? Is it one part contentment, another part pleasure, and a third part exquisite joy? Is it a sensation, a feeling, a thought, or state of mind? Slogans such as "happiness is a warm puppy" cheapen and trivialize the true meaning of happiness.

The biblical word that captures and crystalizes the idea of happiness is *blessedness*. It includes a wholistic satisfaction that touches the soul, the mind, the will, indeed the entire inner person. Beatitude is what we seek.

Blessedness is never an achievement. We cannot earn it, nor can we manipulate it. It is the fruit of divine grace, a gift only God himself is able to bestow upon us. Though we have the capacity to receive it, we are powerless to produce it. Though we are active in its search, we are passive in its reception. Blessedness is something God does *for* us, *to* us, and *in* us.

Blessedness is a matter of degrees. It reaches its zenith in God's final completion of our sanctification, which the Bible calls glorification.

The end of sanctification is glorification:

"Moreover, whom he did predestinate, them he also called: and whom he called, them he also justified: and whom he justified, them he also glorified." (Romans 8:30)

Here the apostle Paul sets forth the "Golden Chain" of the order of salvation (*ordo salutis*). The last link of the chain is glorification, which is the consummation of our sanctification, the ultimate destiny of predestination, the crowning climax to our justification.

The goal of glory was established by God in

eternity. He has appointed us to this end from the foundation of the world. Paul declares:

"And that he might make known the riches of his glory on the vessels of mercy, which he had afore prepared unto glory. . . ." (Romans 9:23)

The Christian is a vessel of mercy, a container filled by divine grace. There is an ultimate purpose to God's plan for us. We are being prepared for something. Preparation is done to ensure the finished product. In this case, the purpose of that preparation is *unto* glory. Glory is the point of completion, the point at which all of the preparations converge into our final state.

The chief aspect of that final glory is the beatific vision of the soul. The theological term for it is the *visio dei*, the soul's vision of God.

The beatific vision of the soul is promised to us initially by Christ in the Sermon on the Mount:

"Blessed are the pure in heart: for they shall see God." (Matthew 5:8)

Each of the beatitudes includes a category of people characterized by a specific virtue, followed by a divine promise of reward. Those that are poor in spirit are promised the kingdom of heaven. Those that mourn are promised comfort. Those that are merciful are promised mercy in return.

The promise of the beatific vision is reserved for those who are pure in heart. But no one in this life ever attains perfect purity of heart. Purity of heart in its perfect manifestation is delayed until heaven. Likewise, our perfect happiness is also delayed.

Purity of heart is an indispensable facet of holiness. It is a necessary ingredient, a prerequisite for the vision of God. The author of Hebrews writes:

"Follow peace with all men, and holiness, without which no man shall see the Lord." (Hebrews 12:14)

Holiness is the "without which" it is impossible to see the Lord.

At present God is invisible to us. This fact perhaps more than any other vexes the Christian. We long to behold the face of God. We ache for a face-to-face relationship with him. For now, however, that is denied us.

The curse God placed upon Cain passes in part to all humanity. Cain groaned at the prospect of his punishment:

"My punishment is greater than I can bear. Behold, thou hast driven me out this day from the face of the earth; and from thy face shall I be hid; and I

shall be a fugitive and a vagabond in the earth. . . ."
(Genesis 4:13-14)

In our inability to perceive the face of God we bear the mark of Cain upon our foreheads. We too are vagabonds, fugitives, and pilgrims. We have been consigned to live east of Eden. We are exiles from paradise, expatriots from our native land. We long to go home, to kiss the earth of Eden and behold our Creator face to face as he walks in the cool of the garden. But though the veil of the temple has been torn for us, and though in Christ we have access to the presence of God, the angel with the flaming sword still guards the entrance to Eden. That sword will not be removed until we gain entrance into heaven.

The angel's sword protects paradise from humans with impure hearts. No person with the slightest impurity can enter that place. We are interlopers in the vicinity of Eden. The God who dwells in light is too holy to even look at iniquity. He will look at us once we are covered by the cloak of Christ's righteousness, but even then he will not remove the veil from his own face until we are glorified.

It is hard to serve and worship an unseen God. We prove the adage "out of sight, out of mind" by our slothful struggle. Yet there is a mixture of kindness in that lack of visibility. Though we long to see him, the vision itself, were it possible, would be fatal to us. For a person with an impure heart to gaze upon the face of God would be to receive the death penalty. God declared to Moses:

"And he said, Thou canst not see my face: for there shall no man see me, and live." (Exodus 33:20)

This warning was given to Moses when he asked to see the glory of God. If there was any saint in the Old Testament who was worthy of seeing the face of God, it was Moses. Moses was the mediator of the Old Covenant, the one through whom the Law was given. He witnessed extraordinary marvels executed by the hand of God. He heard God's voice speak to him out of the burning bush. He saw the plagues fall upon Egypt. He beheld the parting of the Red Sea, and the pillar of cloud and pillar of fire that led the children of Israel in the wilderness.

Still the heart of Moses remained restless. He earnestly sought the beatific vision. Though well along the path of sanctification, he yearned for the final taste of glory and sought its utter fullness. He begged God for the ultimate experience:

"And he said, I beseech thee, show me thy glory. And he said, I will make all my goodness pass before thee, and I will proclaim the name of the LORD before thee; and will be gracious to whom I will be gracious, and will show mercy on whom I will show mercy." (Exodus 33:18-19)

God responded to Moses' request by an act of superlative condescension. He stooped in his mercy to allow Moses to see what mortals are customarily denied. He allowed Moses a glimpse, a backward glance, of his glory:

"And the LORD said, Behold, there is a place by me, and thou shalt stand upon a rock: And it shall come to pass, while my glory passeth by, that I will put thee in a cleft of the rock, and will cover thee with my hand while I pass by: And I will take away mine hand, and thou shalt see my back parts; but my face shall not be seen." (Exodus 33:21-23)

For Moses to see what he saw, certain things had to happen. First, he had to stand in a place *by* God. He had to draw near to God, to come close enough to him to catch a glimpse of glory.

Second, he had to stand upon a rock. Standing in the mud or on the sand is not an appropriate foundation to behold the living God. It is no accident that the rock is a frequent biblical image for Christ. Those who do not stand upon him have no hope of ever seeing God.

The third prerequisite was that Moses be sheltered in the cleft of the rock. Again the image suggests that Christ is our hiding place from the dreadful, piercing eye of God.

The fourth and final prerequisite for the vision was that Moses be covered. In this case, he was covered by the hand of God. In our case, the nakedness of our souls is covered by the atonement of Christ.

After, and only after, these provisions were met did God display his glory to Moses. Even at that it was a limited display. God prevented Moses from a frontal view of divine glory. Moses' vision was restricted to a glimpse of the back parts or, more literally, the "hindquarters" of God. When all was said and done, Moses was not permitted to see the face of God.

Though elsewhere the Bible says Moses spoke to God "face-to-face," the expression does not connote a visual encounter. To say that he spoke face-to-face with God merely indicates that Moses enjoyed a privileged relationship of intimacy and conversation with God. He was allowed a proximity to the divine presence that few were afforded. Though he enjoyed the posture or position of a face-to-face relationship, it did not include a visual apprehension of the face of God.

WHY IS GOD INVISIBLE TO US?

When we use the term *invisible*, we describe that which the eyes cannot perceive. For the eye to perceive objects, necessary conditions must be met. First, we can see nothing without the presence of light. Vision is impotent in utter darkness. Second, to receive a visual image of something there must be a "something" to see. Such an object must have physical properties. The incorporeal, or pure spirit, cannot be seen by the eye.

God is incorporeal. He has no physical properties. Though the Bible speaks of the "face" of God, the term is used figuratively or anthropomorphically. To speak of God's face is to describe him in human terms. In reality, God has no face. He has no lips, nose, eyebrows, forehead, or ears. He is not a man. He is the "immortal, invisible, the only wise God" (1 Timothy 1:17).

Even in heaven, the vision of God is not experienced with the eyes. When Jesus promised that the pure in heart would see God, he did not mean that it would be a physical perception. No optic nerve is potent enough to enable a human being, even a glorified human being, to have a physical perception of the invisible God.

The first reason God is invisible to us, then, is because he is intrinsically invisible. Any visual display of God is a *theophany*, a term which refers to a visible manifestation of the invisible God. In the Old Testament there were several such displays of God's glory: the burning bush, the shekinah glory cloud, and the pillar of fire, to name but a few. These external manifestations of the invisible character of God were indeed visible to human eyes. They represent a breakthrough into the invisible realm made possible by God's condescending grace toward mortals.

But there is a second, perhaps more important, reason God is invisible to us, and it has nothing to do with the limitations of eyesight. Certain material objects exist that are beyond our normal powers of vision. With the aid of technical instruments, however, we are able to see things not visible to the naked eye. The telescope allows us to view things too distant to see without assistance. The microscope enables us to view things too small to see with the naked eye. In both cases the natural strength of our vision is finite.

However, even if God were near enough, big enough, and completely physical in nature, we still would not be able to see him. No scope is powerful enough to bring him into view. This is not because of a limit or defect in our eyes. The deficiency lies with our hearts. It is not because our eyes are not strong enough; it is because our hearts are not pure enough to "see" God.

The promise, then, of the beatific vision is not to those with strong eyes but to those with pure hearts. It is the pure in heart, and only the pure in heart, who receive the beatitudinal promise: "Blessed are the pure in heart; for they shall see God."

The promise Jesus gave in the Beatitudes is echoed and reinforced by the apostle John:

"Behold, what manner of love the Father hath bestowed upon us, that we should be called the sons of God: therefore the world knoweth us not, because it knew him not. Beloved, now are we the sons of God, and it doth not yet appear what we shall be: but we know that, when he shall appear, we shall be like him; for we shall see him as he is. And every man that hath this hope in him purifieth himself, even as he is pure." (1 John 3:1-3)

This extraordinary passage begins with a note of apostolic astonishment that might be called the original chorus of "Amazing Grace." He expresses stark amazement at the incredible extent of the love of God. God's love is so expansive, his mercy so profound, that he actually bestows upon us the unspeakable privilege of being considered his children. No earthly king would ever consider rebellious traitors as candidates for adoption into his royal family. But this is precisely what the Father has done. He has adopted us, who by nature are his sworn enemies, into his family.

The apostle John then moves from what we know for certain to what is uncertain and mysterious to him, and then back again to that which is certain.

In the first instance he declares what is certain immediately. *"Now,"* he writes, "are we the sons of God." That much is sure. He then adds to this certainty what is unknown about the future. "It doth not yet appear what we shall be." God has not given us a complete blueprint showing what our lives will be like in heaven. The Bible offers clues about our future state, but there remains much that is unknown and mysterious to us.

Despite the abiding mysteries regarding our future state, John points to two aspects of heaven that are certain. First, we will be like him. Second, we shall see him as he is. The question this raises is, Whom shall we be like? Is our future conformity likened to the Father or the Son? Is John speaking to us of the appearance of Christ or the appearance of the Father?

The question may place us on the horns of a false dilemma. We remember that Christ is the "brightness of his glory, and the express image of his person" (Hebrews 1:3). To behold the glory of Christ is to behold the glory of God. We also remember that, while it is necessary in our Trinitarian faith to distinguish among the *persons* of the Godhead, the personal distinction is not an *essential* distinction. It is real but not essential in the sense that there is a real personal difference but that the three are one in essence.

However, when the New Testament speaks of his "appearing," it usually has specific reference to the appearance of Christ. Also, the goal of our sanctification is conformity to the image of Christ. When John speaks of being "like him," the natural assumption is that "him" refers to Jesus.

On the other hand, the New Testament also calls us to imitate God the Father in our sanctification. We are to be holy as he is holy. More important, when the word *God* occurs in Scripture in a straightforward, unqualified sense, it almost always refers to the Father. In the text of John itself, God is the antecedent of the word *him*. This compelling point leads me to conclude that John is speaking here of

God the Father, whom we will be like and whom we shall see as he is.

This discussion may seem a matter of quibbling, since to see the essence of Christ is to see the essence of God. I belabor the point because if John is speaking of God the Son, we might infer that the full extent of the beatific vision will be limited to an unveiled view of the incarnate Jesus in his heavenly glory. That would be a glorious experience, to be sure, but it would fall short of seeing the vision of the very essence of deity. It would probably go even beyond what the disciples beheld at the Transfiguration, but it would still fall short of seeing the "face of God."

The church has customarily seen in this text a promise of the vision of the very essence of God. John says that we shall see him *as he is.*

To see God as he is, is to perceive him in his pure, divine essence. The Vulgate translates this text, *in se est.* That is, we will behold the innermost *being* of God.

The final question we face with respect to this text concerns the temporal and causal relationship between becoming like him and seeing him as he is. John says we will be like him because we shall see him as he is. The dilemma is this: Will the beatific vision be the *cause* of our glorification, or will our final glorification be the *condition* for the beatific vision?

Since it is the impurity of our hearts that blocks our vision of God, it would seem necessary that our hearts be purified *before* we can behold him as he is. Remember the sequence of Jesus' beatitude: "Blessed are the pure in heart, for they shall see God." Jesus did not say, "Blessed are those who see God, for they shall be made pure of heart." We also remember the teaching of Hebrews, which says that without holiness no one will see the Lord.

On the surface, at least, it seems fairly clear that glorification will precede the beatific vision and serve as the necessary condition for its possibility.

On the other hand, it is possible to read John's words another way. He may mean that the conclusive act of grace by which our sanctification will be made full, total, and complete is the beatific vision itself. That is, the effect of seeing him as he is will be so dramatic that the experience itself will remove all residual sin from our souls. Seeing him will so flood the human soul with glory that it will expel from us all abiding wickedness.

I'm not sure which of these options is the correct one. I think the weight of Scripture points toward the former rather than the latter, namely, that God will first glorify us so that we may then behold him as he is.

When we speak of the sequence of the acts of glorification and the beatific vision, we must remember that it may not necessarily be a *temporal* one. It may be a *logical* sequence. This means that our glorification may occur at the same moment as the vision of God. Two actions may be simultaneous though one is logically prior to the other. For example, in our doctrine of justification by faith, we recognize that there is no time gap between the presence of our faith and the presence of our justification. At the very moment faith is present, justification is present as well. God does not wait five years, five minutes, or five seconds after we have faith before he declares us justified in Christ. Yet we do not say that faith is *by* justification. Justification is logically dependent upon faith; faith is not logically dependent upon justification. Faith is the necessary condition for justification. Likewise, it seems that glorification is the necessary condition for the beatific vision. It is logically *prior* to the vision though it may occur at the same time.

EDWARDS ON THE BEATIFIC VISION

Jonathan Edwards once preached a sermon on the beatific vision based on the text of Matthew 5:8. In his exposition he argued that the vision of God will not be a physical act:

> It is not any sight with the bodily eyes: the blessedness of the soul does not enter in at that door. This would make the blessedness of the soul dependent on the body, or the happiness of man's superior part dependent on the inferior. . . . It is not any form or visible representation, nor shape, nor colour, nor shining light, that is seen, wherein this great happiness of the soul consists.[1]

Though the vision of God will consist in a spiritual apprehension, this does not mean that we will have no physical vision in heaven. In our resurrected bodies we will be able to enjoy the view of the splendor of Christ:

> The saints in heaven will behold an outward glory as they are in the human nature of Christ, which is united to the Godhead, as it is the body of that person who is God; and there will doubtless be appearances of a divine and immutable glory and beauty in Christ's glorified body, which it will indeed be a refreshing and blessed sight to see.

But the beauty of Christ's body as seen by the bodily eyes, will be ravishing and delightful, chiefly as it will express his spiritual glory.[2]

As sweet and majestic as this vision of the glorified incarnate Christ will be, it is not the ultimate vision of God of which Scripture speaks. Edwards says:

> But to see God is this. It is to have an immediate, sensible, and certain understanding of God's glorious excellency and love.[3]

When Edwards speaks of an "immediate" vision of God, he means a vision that is not mediated through the eyes. It is a direct "seeing" of the mind. He describes at length what the Bible means by "seeing" God. It is called "seeing" God because, as Edwards notes:

> the view will be very direct; as when we see things with the bodily eyes. God will, as it were, immediately discover himself to their minds, so that the understanding shall behold the glory and love of God, as a man beholds the countenance of a friend.[4]

Edwards gives a second reason why the beatific vision is called "seeing":

> It is called seeing because it will be most certain. When persons see a thing with their own eyes, it gives them the greatest certainty they can have of it, greater than they can have by any information of others. So the sight that they will have in heaven will exclude all doubting.[5]

Third, Edwards cites the vivacity of this experience as being as sharp as any earthly reason:

> It is called seeing, because the apprehension of God's glory and love is as clear and lively as when anything is seen with bodily eyes. . . . The saints in heaven will see the glory of the body of Christ after the resurrection with bodily eyes, but they will have no more immediate and perfect way of seeing that visible glory than they will of beholding Christ's divine and spiritual glory. . . . They will behold God in an ineffable, and to us now inconceivable, manner.[6]

Finally, Edwards speaks of the vision of the inner spiritual nature of God:

The intellectual sight which the saints will have of God will make them as sensible of his presence, and give them as great advantages for conversing with him, as the sight of the bodily eyes doth an earthly friend. . . . But their souls will have the most clear sight of the spiritual nature of God itself. They shall behold his attributes and disposition towards them more immediately, and therefore with greater certainty, than it is possible to see any thing in the soul of an earthly friend by his speech and behaviour.[7]

Thus Edwards gives lucid reasons for why the beatific vision is called a vision. It involves a seeing more pure, more comprehensive, and more delightful than earthly vision can behold. He then explains the blessedness that flows from the vision. It is what makes the beatific vision beatific:

First. It yields a delight suitable to the nature of an intelligent creature. . . . Man's reason is, as it were, a heavenly ray, or, in the language of the wise man, it is "the candle of the Lord." It is that wherein mainly consists the natural image of God, it is the noblest faculty of man, it is that which ought to bear rule over the other powers; being given for that end, that it might govern the soul. . . . Intellectual pleasures consist in the beholding of spiritual excellencies and beauties, but the glorious excellency and beauty of God are for the greatest. . . . It is a thing most agreeable to reason that the soul should delight itself in this . . . so that when it is enjoyed, it is with inward peace, and a sweet tranquility of soul.[8]

In the enjoyment of the beatific vision the soul finally reaches the goal of its supreme quest. At last we enter into that haven where we find our peace and rest. The end of restlessness is reached; the warfare between flesh and spirit ends. Peace that transcends anything in this world fills the heart. We reach the heights of excellency and sweetness only dreamed of in this mortal flesh. We shall see him as he is. No veil, no shield will hide his face. The immediate and direct vision will flood the soul from the wellspring on high. The highest joy, the greatest pleasure, the purest delight will be ours without mixture and without end.

One taste of this felicity will erase all painful memories and heal each dreadful wound incurred in this vale of tears. No scar will remain. The pilgrim's progress will be complete. The body of death, the burden of sin, will vaporize the moment we behold his face.

NOTES

Chapter 1
1. *Basic Writings of Saint Augustine*, ed. Whitney J. Oates, vol. 1, *Confessions* (Grand Rapids: Baker, 1948), 3.
2. R. C. Sproul, John Gerstner, and Arthur Lindsley, *Classical Apologetics* (Grand Rapids: Zondervan, 1984), *ix.*

Chapter 2
1. John B. Taylor, *Ezekiel*, Tyndale Old Testament Commentaries, ed. D. J. Wiseman (Downers Grove, Ill.: InterVarsity, 1969), 55.
2. Ibid.
3. Walter Eichrodt, *Ezekiel* (Philadelphia: Westminster, 1970), 57.
4. Keith W. Carley, *The Book of the Prophet Ezekiel*, Cambridge Bible Commentary (Cambridge: Cambridge Univ. Press, 1974), 17.
5. Flavius Josephus, *The Jewish War*, ed. Gaalya Cornfield (Grand Rapids: Zondervan, 1982), 427.

Chapter 3
1. *The Works of Jonathan Edwards*, revised by Edward Hickman, vol. 2 (Carlisle, Pa.: Banner of Truth Trust, 1974), 12.
2. Ibid.
3. As cited by Thomas Aquinas in *Nature and Grace*, LCC XI (Philadelphia: Westminster, n.d.), 138.
4. Edwards.
5. Ibid.
6. Ibid.
7. Ibid.

8. Ibid.
9. Ibid.
10. Ibid., 14.
11. Ibid.
12. Ibid.
13. W. Luijpen, *Fenomenologie En Atheisme*, (Utrecht: Aula-Boeken, 1967), 326.
14. Edwards.
15. Ibid., 15.
16. Ibid., 17.
17. Ibid.

Chapter 4

1. John Calvin, *Institutes of the Christian Religion*, trans. Henry Beveridge, vol. 1 (Grand Rapids: Eerdmans, 1964), 68-69.
2. Ibid., 72.
3. Ibid.
4. Ibid., 84.
5. Ibid., 85.
6. Ibid.
7. Ibid., 72.
8. Ibid., 84.
9. Ibid., 85.
10. Ibid.

Chapter 5

1. A. F. Kirkpatrick, *The Book of Psalms*, Thornapple Commentaries (Grand Rapids: Baker, 1982), 700-702.
2. Ibid., 704.
3. Calvin, 304.
4. Ibid., 303.
5. Ibid., 305.
6. Ibid., 307.

7. Ibid.
8. Ibid.
9. Ibid., 307-8.
10. Ibid., 309.
11. Ibid.
12. Ibid.

Chapter 6
1. See G. C. Berkouwer, *Vaticaans Concilie En Nieuvo Theologie* (Kampen: J. H. Kok, 1964), 274-315.

Chapter 8
1. John Gerstner, *Reasons for Faith* (Grand Rapids: Baker, 1967), 31.
2. René Descartes, *Discourse on Method & Other Writings*, trans. *Wollaston* (London: Penguin, 1968), 164.
3. Ibid., 150f.
4. Immanuel Kant, *The Critique of Pure Reason*, trans. F. Max Muller (Garden City, N.J.: Doubleday, 1966), 194f.
5. Ibid., 255.
6. Augustus Hopkins Strong, *Systematic Theology*, (Old Tappan, N.J.: Revell, 1907), 487.
7. See footnotes to Romans 7 and 1 Corinthians 2:14 in Scofield Reference Bible (New York: Oxford, 1917). For further insight on dispensational theology, see John Gerstner's *Wrongly Dividing the Word of Truth* (Nashville: Wolgemuth and Hyatt, 1991).
8. For similar examples of Churchill's wit see William Manchester, *The Last Lion*, vol. 2 (Boston: Little, Brown, 1983).

Chapter 9
1. See *The Nicene and Post-Nicene Fathers*, ed. Philip Schaff, vol. 3 (Grand Rapids: Eerdmans, 1988), 369.

2. Jonathan Edwards, *On Knowing Christ* (Carlisle, Pa.: Banner of Truth Trust, 1958), 18.
3. Ibid.
4. Ibid., 20.
5. Ibid.
6. Calvin, 97.
7. Karl Barth, *The Epistle to the Romans*, trans. Edwyn C. Hoskyns (London: Oxford Univ. Press, 1933), 53.

Chapter 10
1. John Bunyan, *The Pilgrim's Progress* (Carlisle, Pa.: Banner of Truth Trust, 1977), 3.
2. Ibid.
3. Ibid., 9-10.

Chapter 11
1. *The Works of Jonathan Edwards*, 905-6.
2. Ibid.
3. Ibid.
4. Ibid., 907.
5. Ibid.
6. Ibid.
7. Ibid.
8. Ibid.

INDEX OF SCRIPTURE

255

R. C. Sproul (Drs., Free University of Amsterdam) is the founder and president of Ligonier Ministries, and he serves as senior minister of preaching and teaching at St. Andrews Chapel, Lake Mary, Florida. He is host of the national daily radio program *Renewing Your Mind*, and he speaks at many conferences. He has written more than fifty books, including *The Holiness of God*, *Faith Alone*, *The Hunger for Significance*, and *The King without a Shadow*.